David Stockley has over 30 years' service with the Metropolitan Police. He has been associated with drug investigations over the last 20 years ranging from street use to international trafficking.

He was deputy to the officer in charge of the Central Drug Squad at New Scotland Yard and operational head of the National Drugs Intelligence Unit. During this time he travelled widely on drug enforcement matters in Europe, North and South America and the Caribbean. He also compiled the Metropolitan Police in-service training manual on drugs on which this book was originally based.

O P T I M A

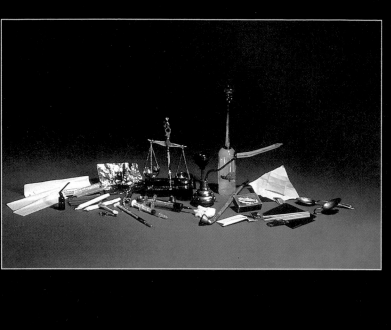

DRUG WARNING

DAVID STOCKLEY

An OPTIMA Book

First published in Great Britain in 1986 by Macdonald & Co. (Publishers) Ltd
This new edition published in 1992 by Optima

Copyright © David Stockley 1986 and 1992
Illustrations copyright © Metropolitan Police 1986 and 1992

The moral right of the author has been asserted.

A CIP catalogue record for this book is available from the British Library.

ISBN 0356 209806

Typeset by Leaper & Gard Ltd, Bristol
Printed and bound in Italy by GRAPHICOM SRL

Optima Books
A Division of
Little, Brown and Company (UK) Limited
165 Great Dover Street
London SE1 4YA

CONTENTS

THE DRUGS

REFERENCE SECTION

FOREWORD

BY THE RIGHT HONOURABLE THE LORD LANE AFC, FORMER LORD CHIEF JUSTICE OF ENGLAND

If someone could stop the abuse of drugs tomorrow, not only would thousands of young people be saved from degradation and possible death, but also one of the main causes for the upsurge in all types of crime would go. It follows that anything which can help us to understand and combat the problems of this new plague before it destroys us is greatly to be welcomed. This remarkable book is designed as a Baedeker to guide the inexperienced traveller in this difficult area. It succeeds in that aim, but unlike so many guide-books it also makes fascinating reading as a narrative.

Every type of drug is examined, its origin, medicinal use, abuse, effect and dangers. Every aspect of the drug scene is explored from the facilities available for treatment for addiction down to the esoteric language of the trade.

There is no-one who would not benefit from reading this book. The author is to be congratulated.

Lane C.J.

ACKNOWLEDGEMENTS

Bringing *Drug Warning* up to date for publication of the second edition has been an onerous task. So much has happened in the drug scene since 1986 when my first book was published. I am therefore indebted to many of my colleagues and friends for their professional advice and assistance. In particular:

Tony Goring, Principal Photographer, Metropolitan Police Photographic Services for updating and adding to the photographic illustrations; Alan MacFarlane, Chief Inspector and John Gerrard, Senior Inspector, Home Office Drugs Branch; Dr Howard Stead BSc, PhD, Drugs Intelligence Laboratory, Forensic Science Service, Aldermaston; Bill Wilson BSc (Pharm), PhD, John Metcalfe BSc, PhD and Diana Sebastion, Metropolitan Police Forensic Science Laboratory; Ric Treble BSc and Jane Pitts CChem, MRSC, Laboratory of the Government Chemist; Ms Michele Verroken, Head of the Doping Control Unit, Sports Council; David Turner, Director, Standing Conference on Drug Abuse; the Law Department, Royal Pharmaceutical Society of Great Britain; and Colleagues in the National Drugs Intelligence Unit and drug squads in police forces throughout the country.

David Stockley, 1992

AUTHOR'S NOTE

Drug abuse is a crisis we can no longer ignore. Once hidden and restricted to sectors of the larger cities, it has now spread throughout the country and to every section of society.

It is seen in drug-related deaths, addiction, crime and disorder. It has surfaced in our schools, colleges, places of entertainment, in sport and in the workplace. On our housing estates, drugs have taken hold to breed their own sub-culture, devastating families and involving even the very young.

In 1980 just over 38 kilograms of heroin were seized in Great Britain. Since then annual seizures increased dramatically through the decade to over 600 kilograms in 1990. This was accompanied by a tragic rise in the number of addicts. Other illegal and dangerous drugs are also now more widely and cheaply available than ever before.

At first the many warnings from the police and from others involved in counselling and treatment mainly went unheeded. While passing public interest might have been caught by the odd, sensational newspaper headline, the overall attitude remained, 'It couldn't happen here'. It has – and it is getting worse!

Law enforcement alone, however, is not the solution. The police aim to protect and assist the citizen in maintaining a peaceful society. This is rooted in consultation and co-operation at community level, and in close liaison with workers in health, educational and other social agencies. Through this multi-agency approach, all the caring agencies, including the police, should work together to educate, advise and, where necessary, support and rehabilitate.

The police were keen to play their full part in the local community by informing the public about the various drugs, their appearance, effects and dangers. This was initially satisfied by police officers experienced in the field giving regular talks and presentations to neighbourhood groups and local organisations. But as the worsening drugs situation became more apparent, demand for these outgrew qualified human resources.

It was clear that the public wanted accurate and up-to-date information about this growing problem. Because of this, in 1985 I compiled the Metropolitan Police Drug Education Pack. It was intended as an in-service training aid for Community Liaison Officers, a factual package with slides to cover presentations to young people, whether in school or not, to parents, teachers and youth club leaders, and to other interested professional or social groups.

The launch of the Education Pack brought a dramatic response. We were inundated with requests from outside organisations and individuals for a copy. Through the first edition of *Drug Warning* we attempted to meet this clear need for objective information about drugs and their abuse. Five years on with the publication of this second edition, it is sad to say that this need is even greater.

In the meantime the Government has developed a comprehensive strategy for tackling drug misuse. Co-ordinated by the Home Office with a Minister of State having responsibility for drug misuse policy, the strategy involves simultaneous action in five main areas:

- Improving international co-operation in order to reduce supplies from abroad.
- Increasing the effectiveness of police and customs enforcement.
- Maintaining effective deterrents and tight domestic controls.
- Developing prevention publicity and education.
- Improving treatment and rehabilitation.

Of particular relevance has been the launch of a major *health education and information publicity campaign,* much of which has targeted young people at risk. Initially tackling the dangers of heroin misuse, it has been extended to drug misusers in general and injectors in particular. There has been great emphasis on the dangers of contracting and spreading HIV (Human Immunodeficiency Virus) and AIDS (Acquired Immune Deficiency Syndrome) through sharing contaminated injecting equipment. In support of this has been the establishment of a national network of outlets for used syringe and needle exchange and disposal, together with detailed guidance on cleaning injecting equipment for those who are unable or unwilling to obtain new and sterile equipment.

A *wider range of treatment options* are being developed (details on pages 175–179). Backed up by community advice and counselling services and community drug teams, 'outreach workers' seek out drug misusers with the object of drawing them into a treatment regime, part of which would include help and advice on reducing the risk of HIV infection.

Funds have been made available to encourage the development of *drugs education* in schools, colleges and the youth service. This has enabled local authorities in England to appoint Drugs Education Co-ordinators to promote and co-ordinate drugs education and to provide training for teachers and youth workers. Similar projects have been established in Scotland and Wales. Health education, which includes drug, alcohol and solvent misuse, as well as information about the dangers associated with smoking and AIDS has also become an important element in the new National Curriculum in England and Wales.

The Home Office *drugs prevention initiative* has been established to promote the prevention of drugs misuse. Locally based teams are being set up in selected areas which are judged most at risk from drug misuse. The teams, supported by a Central Drugs Prevention Unit, take account of health, education, community and legal interests in relation to drugs misuse and prevention. They build on current ongoing local initiatives and encourage the active participation of statutory and voluntary organisations. Local involvement by interested parties including parents' and tenants' groups, employers, churches and religious groups and the media is sought to contribute to the development and implementation of local drugs prevention measures.

An increasing number of drugs offenders are being cautioned by the police (see page 159) for simple possession cases instead of being prosecuted. This deliberate diversion from the criminal courts is underpinned by a referral system which is being adopted by more and more police forces. The procedure allows the police to offer people arrested for drug offences the opportunity to obtain independent and confidential advice on drugs problems with the aim, where necessary, of voluntary admission into a treatment programme.

For those who appear before a court, current sentencing strategy is moving towards the provision of credible and demanding community sentences for offenders who do not need to be sentenced to custody. The Criminal Justice Act 1991 contains a new provision specifically aimed at drug (and alcohol) misusing offenders. It enables sentencers, subject to certain criteria, to attach to a probation order a requirement that the offender undergoes treatment for drug or alcohol dependency. This condition may only be imposed with the offender's consent. The treatment may be residential or non-residential.

There are many other initiatives, both local and national, which contribute to the overall UK drugs strategy. A detailed account can be found in a publication produced for the Home Office by the Central Office of Information entitled *UK Action on Drug Misuse – The Government's Strategy*.

Drug Warning is intended to complement these various initiatives. It is a practical guide on identification and recognition of all the different drugs which have potential for misuse or are currently being misused. With the help of full-colour photographs, the book describes what each drug looks like, gives details of how it is taken, outlines the possible effects and dangers, the symptoms to look out for and the equipment and paraphernalia associated with the drug.

Drug abuse is not an easy subject, and there are no short cuts or simple methods to identify suspected substances or users. I don't attempt to advise parents on how to deal with a child who may be abusing drugs or employers on the policy which they should adopt within their organisation. This is best done by those more qualified in the field. Various national organisations which offer expert help and advice are listed in the reference section (pages 170–174).

Most common substances which are misused or have the potential for misuse are included in the book. But it must not be assumed that because something is absent, it does not have potential for misuse.

Some medical preparations have become more readily identifiable to the general public because of the well-known brand name by which they were prescribed. This is changing as doctors should now generally prescribe drugs by their non-proprietary or generic titles if they are available. This gives pharmacists some flexibility to dispense any suitable product they have in stock. It may also be less expensive for the NHS. The only exception is where alternative preparations do not suit the patient and a change would cause adverse effects.

As a result of these changes, the number of generic products have increased but there is no obligation on different manufacturers to produce identical looking products. Some look very similar, others are quite different. Consequently visual identification of some types of drugs is much more difficult. Where non-proprietary products are available, a sample is shown together with a well-known proprietary brand. It would be impracticable to attempt to produce a totally comprehensive display as the range available is constantly changing. It does, however, demonstrate clearly the inherent problems in relying too heavily on visual identification. Approximate sizes of illustrated drugs are also shown. Where a drug comes in various strengths, the size of the tablet or capsule may vary accordingly.

This book is directed primarily at parents, teachers and employers, but **young people** in particular will respect the truth about the relative dangers of different drugs. They are entitled to know the facts so that they can make their own decisions.

Parents too must learn to cope with a world where drugs are readily available to their children. They should be aware what drugs look like, what they do and where to go for help and advice.

Teachers and other adults working closely with children can profoundly influence the child's decision. If they are familiar with the substances that circulate in the playground or youth club they can act positively, by example and informed persuasion, to discourage use.

Employers must also consider how they are going to cope with drugs in the workplace. They should think carefully about developing a policy for identifying and dealing with individuals who may be misusing drugs.

Employers are generally responsible for the actions of their employees during the course of their employment. This is particularly pertinent if the job entails the safety and well-being of the public, but the duty also extends to providing a safe working environment for the whole of the workforce.

Two things in particular should be clear to anyone reading *Drug Warning*. One is the vast number of substances that are being abused at street level. The other is that if an individual's behaviour is out of character or causing concern, the possibility of drug misuse must be considered. It is an unfortunate fact that we should all be more conscious of the problem, and when circumstances call for it – THINK DRUGS!

David Stockley, 1992

INTRODUCTION

WHAT IS A DRUG?

Any chemical substance that brings about a change in a person's emotional state, body functioning or behaviour may be termed a drug. This definition includes many substances that might not immediately be considered as drugs.

For most people, 'drugs' means the vast range of pharmaceutical products that are currently available and continue to be developed. They are produced for specific medical purposes and are invaluable in treating all manner of complaints, illnesses and disease. They are widely used to reduce pain and suffering, to stimulate or induce sleep, and to counteract anxiety, tension, nervous disorder and depression.

Properly prescribed the benefits are immeasurable. Such legitimate and laudable use must be distinguished from the illegal, non-medical use of the same substances. However, this distinction becomes blurred when we consider our reliance on drugs of all kinds – just to keep going through the day or to try to improve or change the way we feel.

Alcohol and tobacco are examples of everyday drugs which clearly affect mood, behaviour and the functioning of the body. Alcohol depresses the central nervous system, removing inhibitions and relaxing the user. Smoking brings an immediate and satisfying stimulation, at the same time reducing stress and tension. Though legal, both drugs are often abused and can result in serious mental and physical conditions.

Virtually everybody drinks tea or coffee. Many people rely on the 'pick-me-up' effect of the traditional cup of tea or the stimulating effect of a cup of coffee. One of the most welcome things after a tiresome or exerting activity is a refreshing 'cuppa'. Tea and coffee breaks are built into a day's routine, and both drinks are consumed regularly to revive and give energy. It is the caffeine, a mild stimulant found in both, which gives this needed 'lift'.

Drugs are often taken without thinking, even without realising it. The many remedies for minor stomach disorders or simple headaches, obtainable not only from a community pharmacy but also from supermarkets and other shops, and the way these products are advertised, reflect society's acceptance and need for drugs of all kinds.

Many would consider a visit to their family doctor incomplete without receiving a prescription. The distinction between the beneficial and harmful use becomes even more blurred when doctors are suspected of unnecessarily or overprescribing certain drugs.

With society's widespread tolerance and use of drugs, it is little wonder that some feel the need to experiment with them, trying to find new experiences and excitement, or merely seeking to solve problems and cope with our complex society.

This book is not concerned with the harmless cup of tea, or with cigarettes or headache cures, though these can be dangerously abused. It is about those illicit drugs which circulate at street level, and the pharmaceutical drugs which may be used non-medically, usually for the satisfying sensations they bring.

TYPES OF DRUGS

Drugs come in all kinds of shapes, sizes and compositions. As a result, visual identification is never certain and only laboratory analysis can be considered definite.

Drugs have been categorised in many ways – hard and soft; natural and synthetic; 'uppers' and 'downers'; addictive and non-addictive. Often such divisions cut across each other, or are misleading. The popular media description of 'hard' and 'soft', for example, is neither legal nor scientific.

The most satisfactory division, followed in this book, is by a drug's effects and chemical composition. The groups are:

ANALGESICS – Either derived from opium or synthetically produced, some of these pain-killers are extremely powerful and highly addictive. They include morphine, heroin and methadone, and are a major problem.

DEPRESSANTS – A range of sleeping tablet and anxiety-relievers are abused. They have an effect comparable to that of alcohol. Barbiturates, which have an extremely strong dependence potential, are declining in importance. They have been replaced by benzodiazepines which are now the most commonly prescribed drugs in this group.

STIMULANTS – Cocaine and the amphetamines are the main stimulants, keeping the user awake, alert and excited. Regular consumption can easily bring psychological dependence. Cocaine is increasingly fashionable, and dangerous. Methylenedioxymethylamphetamine (MDMA), the drug known as 'Ecstasy', is included in this group as it is related to the amphetamines although it also has hallucinogenic properties.

HALLUCINOGENS – The most unpredictable group of drugs, including LSD and 'magic mushrooms' (psilocybin), distort perception and induce hallucinations. While not known to cause addiction, they can produce traumatic psychological effects.

CANNABIS – This is the most widespread drug of abuse in Britain and probably the world. It is usually smoked, producing a sickly-sweet smell, and brings to the user a relaxed euphoria. It can cause erratic behaviour and bronchial problems.

SOLVENTS – Various household items, from glues to aerosols and paint-strippers, intoxicate when inhaled causing disorientation. Especially used by young people, they can result in dependence or even death by suffocation or choking.

MISCELLANEOUS – A number of different types of drugs which either do not fit comfortably into any of the previous groups or span a number of them. They include anabolic steroids, 'over-the-counter drugs' (OTC) for example, mild opioid analgesics, laxatives and alkyl nitrites.

HOW DRUGS ARE TAKEN

Drugs can be swallowed, smoked, injected, sniffed or inhaled, and also absorbed through the mucous membranes of the anus or vagina. How a drug is taken will affect the intensity and speed at which it works.

The drug enters the bloodstream, either directly or through the stomach, lungs or body passages. Some act locally, but others are carried to the brain causing messages to be sent through the nerve system, backwards and forwards from the brain to the various parts of the body. The resulting physiological and mental changes are influenced both by what the person sees, hears, smells and touches, and also by his general mood and expectations. The overall effects of taking a drug can vary widely, depending on the type and quantity of drug consumed, the method of administration, how the person feels, where they are and whom they are with.

If individual drugs are taken with alcohol or mixed with other drugs, their effects may be enhanced. Overdosing then becomes more likely and effective and appropriate medical attention more difficult to achieve.

DEPENDENCE, TOLERANCE AND ADDICTION

With repeated consumption a compulsion can develop to continue taking a drug. This is known as dependence, and may be psychological or physical.

Most widespread is *psychological dependence*. This occurs when a person acquires such a strong desire for the sensations the drug brings – such as elation, euphoria, stimulation, sedation, hypnosis, hallucinations or heightened perception – that the drugged state is preferred to normality.

Repeated usage may then follow in order to maintain the experience until any attempt to give up the drug results in severe depression. In some cases, the body adapts and builds a resistance to the drug. When such *tolerance* has set in, the size of the dose has to be progressively increased just to achieve the same effect.

Taking some drugs over long periods causes actual changes in the body until it cannot physically perform if the drug is stopped. Without continued administration the person becomes ill and experiences withdrawal symptoms, and with time increased dosages are often necessary. This is *physical dependence*.

Addiction is the term often used to describe an established dependence on a drug which has serious consequences for the individual and a detrimental effect on society. It may be either psychological or physical. Because the word 'addiction' is considered rather emotive, experts now tend not to use the word or the term 'drug addict'.

Withdrawal from physical dependence can be painful and dangerous, with symptoms ranging from nausea to coma. Particular symptoms are described under the various drug headings. Addiction can often only be cured by lengthy and specialised treatment, for example through a 'weaning-off' process using substitute drugs.

THE DANGERS OF DRUG ABUSE

All drugs, both legal and illegal, carry inherent dangers, and these vary a great deal according to the actual drug misused. Also, because of the physical and psychological differences between individuals, some drugs will have very little effect on one person but will seriously affect another.

Certain risks, however, are general to all drug misuse. The effect of mixing alcohol with other drugs, especially other depressants, has already been mentioned. Doubling up on any drugs may cause adverse reactions and increase the risk of harm. Sometimes a relatively safe dose of each individual drug may combine to result in a fatal overdose – even with readily available over the counter medicines.

Abstinence from drug-taking may ironically bring its own risks. If a user returns to drug misuse on the same dose after tolerance to the drug has declined, the result may be an inadvertent overdose.

Buying drugs at street level is a hazardous practice. Most dealers care little about the quality of the drugs, or what substances have been mixed with them. Heroin, cocaine and amphetamine in particular are frequently 'cut' with other materials, often impure and sometimes poisonous, which are added to increase the volume and so the profits.

Even tablets and capsules offered as pharmaceutical products may not be what they appear. 'Look-alike' drugs are sometimes sold as the real thing, and capsules easily come apart so that the powder inside can be substituted.

On the other hand the drug may be too pure – a user who is accustomed to diluted supplies may underestimate the strength of the drug and so take an overdose.

Injecting drugs is the most direct and potentially most dangerous form of administration. It increases the risks of both dependence and overdose. It also invites the danger of contracting life-threatening infections, such as hepatitis and HIV progressing to AIDS, from dirty and shared syringes.

Capsules can easily be pulled apart, allowing the powder inside to be replaced with something else. Note the quantity of powder which comes from just one capsule

The spread of the HIV infection presents a tremendous problem for society and much attention has been devoted to it by the Government, health authorities and drug agencies to change the behaviour of drug users away from high-risk practices such as sharing syringes. Unfortunately this dangerous practice continues despite a nationwide publicity campaign and a developing network of outlets where used syringes and needles may be exchanged for new.

By sharing, drug users may infect each other and, if they are sexually active and do not practise safe sex, they may transmit HIV to the wider community – both heterosexual and homosexual. HIV infection is spreading although the overall extent is not known. It may be a number of years before the full effects of the problem are felt.

Syringe and needle hygiene is therefore imperative and a clear message must be: **DON'T SHARE – USE ONLY NEW STERILE EQUIPMENT.**

However, to reduce harm among drug users and hence protect society, almost contradictory advice must be given: **IF SHARING DOES TAKE PLACE, ENSURE THE EQUIPMENT IS PROPERLY CLEANSED BEFORE USE.**

Experts recommend that the best method is to boil the equipment. This may damage some syringes. The next best methods are:

- To flush *cold* water and washing up liquid through the syringe or;
- To flush concentrated bleach through the syringe or;
- To use both and;
- Repeat the process several times and;
- Rinse the equipment through with cold water.

It is important that warm water is not used initially as this may cause clotting and prevent complete blood removal.

Users are also advised to rinse the syringe *immediately* with cold water after injecting. This simple precaution will remove most of the blood left in the syringe before it dries. Further information can be obtained from the agencies detailed on pages 168–172.

It is also important that used syringes and needles are disposed of safely. Drugs agencies, syringe and needle exchange centres and some pharmacies keep a 'sharps' bin for used equipment. It is unacceptable to merely discard these items in public areas, particularly where children could be injured and even infected.

Injecting powders and crushed tablets which are not meant for such use is also very dangerous and can cause infections, abscesses and even gangrene at the site of the injections. Undissolved particles injected into a vein are another hazard as they may be carried to the heart and lungs.

Capsules containing drugs in liquid form are also broken open and the contents injected. In an attempt to prevent this, gel-filled capsules have been introduced. However, users have found that they could also inject the gel after treating it in a certain way. Both the liquid and the gel are unsuitable for injection, and the gel in particular could cause serious blood circulation problems.

It is quite wrong to think that sniffing or smoking heroin, rather than injecting it, will avoid the development of both a physical and a psychological dependence. If a drug is by nature addictive then, however it is taken, regular use is likely to lead to dependence.

The effects of drugs can be unpredictable and even the opposite of what is expected. The mood of the user may bring out anxiety, tension and aggressiveness, though the drug is intended to depress the central nervous system (as happens, for example, with alcohol or tranquil-lisers). While generally thought to relax and calm people down, by removing inhibitions they can cause aggressive or violent reactions.

The use of psychoactive drugs (those which affect the mind), even in small doses, can dull psychomotor skills and diminish a person's ability in simple everyday tasks. Driving a motor vehicle or using powered machinery when under the influence of this type of drug can be especially perilous.

There are social and criminal dangers too. By handling or using illegal drugs, a person is liable to prosecution. Drugs are expensive, so there may be an additional temptation to sell some on for profit, thus committing a more serious offence. Many regular users have to resort to crimes such as burglary to finance their habit. There is a tendency, therefore, for users who circulate in the drugs scene to be drawn into a generally criminal way of life.

All these dangers derive from the intentional misuse of drugs. But serious accidents also occur when pharmaceutical drugs fall by mistake into the hands of children and young people. Drugs must always be kept in a safe place. While the security containers in which most tablets, capsules and some mixtures are dispensed reduce the risk, some very young children seem to specialise in opening anything they are not meant to.

Tablets and capsules come in various shapes, sizes and colours, and some look remarkably like sweets. Children can be easily attracted by a bright colour or familiar shape and make a terrible mistake. The photograph overleaf shows the problem only too clearly.

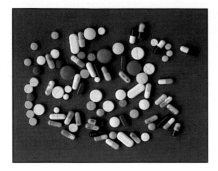

With brightly coloured tablets and capsules, even adults may be deceived. Can you, for example, with any certainty, differentiate between the drugs and the sweets in this picture?

WARNING SIGNS

Parents often ask, 'How can I detect if my child is using or experimenting with drugs?' and 'What signs should I be looking for?' There is no simple answer.

Many of the attitudes and forms of behaviour associated with drug-taking could be confused with the difficult process of just growing up. Occasionally drug users are even more difficult to detect, unless they are discovered actually taking or under the influence of drugs.

The plain fact, as stated in a speech at the Annual Conference of the British Medical Association in 1984, is that 'for the first time in this country there is no such place as a drug-free environment'. Although the majority of young people do not take drugs, the temptation is all around them. It cannot be ignored. Parents must be aware and informed about the availability and dangers of different drugs.

The effects of individual drugs are detailed in the pages starting on page 27. But there are several general signs which may appear out of character for the child and indicate drug abuse:

- Loss of appetite.
- Being either unusually sleepy or unable to sleep at night.
- Bouts of talkative, excitable and overactive behaviour.
- Being unusually irritable, aggressive and even violent.
- Changing moods, from happy and bright to moody and confused, for no apparent reason.
- Telling lies or acting secretively.
- Losing interest in schoolwork and truanting.

- Changing friendship patterns.
- Losing interest in hobbies and sport.
- Money or valuables disappearing from the home.
- Coming to the notice of the police for unruly, disorderly behaviour or dishonesty.
- Unusual spots, sores and marks on the body, arms or around the mouth and nose.
- Stains and chemical smells on clothing and about the body.

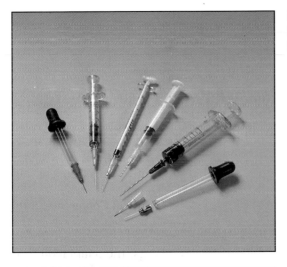

Syringes and needles for injecting drugs, including heroin

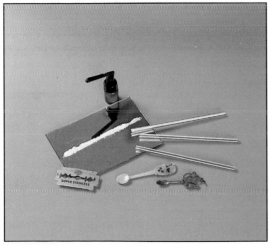

Small mirror, razor and straws associated with 'snorting' (sniffing) cocaine. Also cocaine spoons and container

Homemade cigarettes containing cannabis – known as 'joints' or 'reefers'. Also an ordinary cigarette impregnated with a line of cannabis oil

Bloodstained cotton wool – evidence that a drug such as heroin may have been injected

Employers too must accept that sooner or later they will experience drug misuse amongst their staff. With the problem becoming so widespread across the country a proportion of misusers will be in work. Studies of known drug misusers indicate that at least 30 per cent are in employment.

The implications for an employer are enormous, not only from the likely effect on the individual's performance and time lost through absenteeism, but also the vulnerable position that the individual may place the employer with the workforce, customers and even the public. The legal implications are covered briefly on pages 21 and 24–25.

However, the owners or senior management of an organisation are often too remote from the employees to detect drug-misuse problems. It is therefore important that there is awareness at appropriate levels of the organisation so that section heads can bring early signs of such behaviour to notice through their line management. This means establishing a recognised structure for handling this and other health-related matters – including adequate training.

As in the case with children, drug misuse can be very difficult to identify. Many individuals have been dependent on drugs for a number of years and have managed to continue in employment

without it becoming known. Few will admit to their dependency, particularly if they believed that it would put their jobs at risk.

Finally, attitude and behavioural problems sometimes associated
with drug misuse may be caused by totally unrelated physical, psychological and domestic factors, and even by drink-related problems.

Many of the signs indicating drug misuse in children apply equally
to adults in a working environment. Additional indicators may be:

- Frequent absences from work.
- Above average sick record.
- Poor time keeping.
- Leaving work early.
- Spending too much time away from the allocated work position.
- Visiting the cloakroom on an excessive number of occasions.
- Taking extended coffee or tea breaks.
- Declining or variable and unreliable work performance.
- Impaired memory and an inability to maintain concentration.
- Periods of withdrawal and depression.
- Poor interpersonal skills.
- Hostile to advice or criticism.
- Complaints from working colleagues.
- Borrowing money – always seems to be short of money.
- Decline in personal hygiene.
- Tendency to be accident/incident prone.

In addition to signs and symptoms which may indicate drug misuse,
there will almost certainly be the presence of strange powders, tablets,
capsules and other substances. Depending on what drug is being used
and how it is taken, these will be accompanied by various items of
drugs paraphernalia which enable the user to administer the drug.
They include:

- Scorched tinfoil, tinfoil tubes and matchbox covers.
- Syringes and needles.
- Scorched spoons, ligatures and citric acid.
- Small mirror, razor and straws.
- Tiny spoons (sometimes ornate) and small containers.
- Cigarette papers and homemade cigarettes.
- Bloodstained cotton wool or other material.

- Soft drink cans, glass and plastic bottles, glass tubes, butane gas torch, lighter, matches and perforated tinfoil.
- Square folds of paper which may contain powder.
- Cling film, tinfoil and small self-sealing plastic bags used to package small quantities of drugs.

Once the problem is identified, employers must then decide how to deal with the individual concerned. Managing this situation would be so much easier if thought is given to the matter before the problem occurs. This approach could complement current drug treatment philosophy as the workplace would provide further opportunities both to identify drug abusers and to draw them into a treatment programme. If caught early enough the organisation might be able to keep the employee, thus retaining the skills and training invested in him.

There are many useful briefing documents on developing such a policy and a number of agencies willing to offer advice. (page 174)

Probably one of the most frequent dangers of drug misuse in the workplace is just not being prepared.

Scorched tinfoil, tinfoil tubes and matchbox covers, evidence of smoking heroin – or 'chasing the dragon'

Scorched spoons in which heroin has been dissolved with citric acid (or lemon juice). Also a ligature to make the veins stand out for easier injection

Soft drink cans, bottles, glass tubes, tinfoil and heating sources could mean that cocaine is being smoked

Street 'deals' — pieces of paper carefully folded to contain heroin, cocaine or amphetamine

An alternative means of packaging cocaine 'crack'

THE SITUATION TODAY

Throughout human history there have been isolated accounts of drug misuse, usually associated with bohemian and artistic circles. But it did not become a matter of serious public concern until the late 1950s. Since then it has mushroomed inexorably, with an ever-increasing variety and quantity of drugs available.

HEROIN – This continues to be the single most serious concern today with the vast majority of addicts notified to the Home Office being dependent on it. Thirty-five years ago there were only a handful of addicts, mainly as a result of some organic or medical condition. Illicit, non-therapeutic use of heroin began to grow as a very small number of doctors overprescribed to addicts who then passed on their supplies.

Controls in the 1960s restricted heroin-prescribing to doctors specially licensed by the Home Office. Though overprescribing of heroin substitutes has since emerged, the main source of refined heroin has now switched to other parts of the world.

In recent years we have seen the rise and decline of Chinese heroin (still occasionally found), heroin from Iran and latterly the tremendous impact of Pakistan as a supplier to the whole Western world. Drug abuse is no longer a national problem alone, but must be viewed from a worldwide perspective.

Seizures, most of them still from the Indian Sub-continent and particularly from Pakistan and Afghanistan, are rising at a very fast rate. With Turkey becoming the principal transit country and the Balkan route through east European countries the conduit for transporting heroin to the West, there seems little hope of an improvement in present trends. And it has been claimed that as little as a tenth of the heroin smuggled into this country is detected. The switch from injecting to smoking and sniffing during the mid-1980s effectively removed the fear of the needle, particularly amongst new users, and contributed to the increase. Meanwhile over 8,000 new addicts were notified in 1991 – an annual rise of 16 per cent – and 6,300 of those were addicted to heroin.

COCAINE – This is also a growing cause for concern. South American dealers, having captured the American market have now turned their attention to Europe. The quantity of cocaine seized in this country has risen dramatically over the last few years. Although totals have fluctuated, the quantity seized for 1990 equalled that of heroin at around 600 kilograms and the provisional seizure figure for 1991 shows a further rise to almost 1,100 kilograms.

It is not just the soaring quantity of available cocaine that is a worry, but the way it is consumed. The practice which originated in the USA of smoking crack (a form of base cocaine which has a high abuse potential) is increasing here, while mixing cocaine with heroin in a 'speedball' is also occurring. This could result in a highly dangerous dual addiction.

AMPHETAMINE – Abuse emerged in the early 1960s, mostly among young people in the clubs of London and other larger cities. It is very cheap to buy on the street and its use has now become widely established across the country. Amphetamine and cocaine are both stimulants and the effects of these drugs are similar. Because of this it is believed that a ready market is being prepared for cocaine if that too becomes as readily available and as cheap to buy as amphetamine.

Although much amphetamine is imported, more is being home-produced in backroom factories. Its manufacture requires only a basic knowledge of chemistry and very little apparatus.

Methylamphetamine is closely related to amphetamine although certain of its effects are more pronounced. Seizures fluctuate quite considerably. It reached a peak in 1989 but since then it has not been quite as prominent. When available it is often sold as good quality amphetamine and users may not be aware of the added dangers involved. Smokable methylamphetamine or 'ice', which is widely abused in the USA with serious consequences, has briefly made an appearance in this country.

Other drugs are on the increase too. LSD (Lysergic Acid Diethylamide), which faded from fashion in the late 1970s has made a significant comeback in recent years. This was mainly associated with the 'acid house' or 'pay party' phenomenon which emerged during 1988–89 and involved large numbers of young people meeting in warehouses or other unoccupied commercial premises – often without permission. Recent information indicates that local 'raves', which took over from the acid house or pay parties, are still widespread across the country and an outlet for the supply of illicit substances.

Demand for LSD is still high and its use now appears to have also moved into public houses, discos and clubs. The drug methylenedioxymethylamphetamine (MDMA) better known as 'ecstasy' received a great deal of media attention during 1989 and the upward trend in abuse of the drug at the time mirrored that of LSD. Quantities of ecstasy seized in 1989 and 1990 were similar at about

40,000 dose units. But provisional seizure figures for 1991 show a massive rise to 252,000 dose units. The increasing misuse of this drug, its toxic effects and unpredictability are currently causing a great deal of concern.

MDMA is an amphetamine-type drug which also has hallucinogenic effects. Amphetamine and LSD, or a mixture of the two, have been sold as ecstasy and some ecstasy seizures have also been found to contain LSD. The three drugs amphetamine, LSD and MDMA have recently been referred to as the 'dance drugs' and are said to be strongly linked to the 'rave' youth culture. Methylenedioxyamphetamine (MDA), a drug which is chemically related to MDMA, also appeared on the UK drug scene during the last few months of 1991.

CANNABIS – This remains the most widely abused illicit drug satisfying a growing user market.

More pharmaceutical drugs are getting on to the black market, either by theft from legitimate sources, by using stolen and forged prescriptions, or through doctors overprescribing. In some cases addicts are receiving an additional supply of drugs by obtaining prescriptions from more than one doctor.

The drug scene is constantly changing, from area to area, and from day to day. Probably the most important factor is the relative availability of individual substances, particularly for first-time or inexperienced experimenters.

Agency workers have found that young drug abusers do not keep to one substance, but will try whatever is readily available. One must therefore anticipate the likelihood of multi-drug abuse, rather than thinking in terms of one or two specific substances.

Taken as a whole, the situation is already alarming with almost 21,000 addicts notified to the Home Office in 1991. It is also accepted that this number is probably only a small proportion of the number of regular misusers of opiates and cocaine. Research has indicated that there could be a five-fold underestimate. Persons found guilty, cautioned or dealt with by compounding (see page 158) for drugs offences topped 44,900 in 1990. Distribution has also been spreading from the city centres to suburbs and rural areas.

The first line of defence in the fight against drugs is HM Customs and Excise who are responsible for preventing drugs coming into or leaving the country. It is the job of the police to prevent drug trafficking or dealing inside the country. Frequently the two combine in joint operations.

The police tackle the problem according to the level on the distribution system, which can best be described as a pyramid. At the top are the major importers and traffickers, especially those who have connections with organised crime. They are dealt with by experienced Drug Squad officers attached to Regional Crime Squads.

Middle-level dealers, who generally remain in one geographical location but serve a multitude of outlets, are handled by force drug and crime squads. Individual users and dealers are the responsibility of uniformed beat officers and CID officers at a local level.

Superimposed upon the law enforcement structure are specialist police and Customs financial investigation teams which enquire into the wealth derived by criminals from drug trafficking.

Drugs intelligence is co-ordinated by the National Drugs Intelligence Unit. Although located in New Scotland Yard, it is staffed by officers from all parts of the country, by Customs and by foreign law enforcement officers. Similarly British Drug Liaison Officers are posted to other countries which have a strategic relevance to the United Kingdom. The Intelligence Unit receives, analyses and passes on intelligence, including financial information, both from within this country and abroad.

The present drugs intelligence system is currently being absorbed into a more efficient framework known as the National Criminal Intelligence Service. This will draw together all relevant information regarding the activities of major criminals involved in serious crime, including drug trafficking.

But the police, and the many other agencies involved, can only make a real impact on the rising level of drug abuse if there is a desire by the community as a whole to reduce the problem – by providing information, for example, which could assist in the arrest of local drug dealers or importers. The police would far prefer this information to come confidentially on a 'face to face' basis, but most police areas can receive information anonymously on special 24-hour answerphones.

Drug abuse, and the need for a concerted effort by every member of the public to rid society of it, was aptly summed up by the Home Secretary in 1983. It still applies today:

'Drug abuse is a disease from which no country and no section of modern society seems immune. It brings ruthless, hardened criminals and weak, self-indulgent users together in a combination which is potentially lethal for good order and civilised values. Stamping it out will be slow and painful. It requires co-operation between governments, law enforcement agencies, professionals, schools and families. The rewards are great if we succeed – and the price of ultimate failure is unthinkable.'

DRUGS AND THE LAW

It is only possible here to give a brief, simple summary of the laws concerning illicit drugs. If detailed information is needed, a solicitor, Release or one of the other organisations listed in the reference section (pages 170–174) should be consulted.

Importing and exporting controlled drugs comes primarily under the jurisdiction of HM Customs and Excise. In either case, the maximum penalty for certain types of drugs is life imprisonment. (Customs and Excise Management Act 1979.)

Customs Officers also have the power to 'compound' offences at ports of entry in respect of individuals unlawfully bringing small quantities of drugs into the country. This is an administrative disposal whereby the person agrees to pay a fixed penalty in lieu of prosecution. If he disputes the offence or refuses to pay the penalty the case would be put before a Magistrates' Court in the normal way.

Within the United Kingdom the most important drugs laws are the Misuse of Drugs Act 1971 together with the Misuse of Drugs Regulations made under the Act, and the Medicines Act 1968.

The Misuse of Drugs Act 1971 divides controlled drugs into three categories, classes A, B and C. They are classified according to their degree of harmfulness or danger, both to the individual and to society at large, with penalties varying accordingly.

* *CLASS A* – Includes opium, morphine, diamorphine (heroin), dipipanone, methadone, dextromoramide, pethidine, cocaine, lysergide (LSD) and phencyclidine. Class B drugs which are prepared for injection are also included.
* *CLASS B* – Includes codeine, amphetamine, methylamphetamine, cannabis and cannabis resin, barbiturates and dihydrocodeine.
* *CLASS C* – Includes buprenorphine, diethylpropion, mazindol, pemoline, phentermine and most benzodiazepines.

The Act provides the police with powers to stop and search persons, vehicles or vessels; to obtain search warrants to search premises; to seize anything which appears to be evidence of an offence; and to arrest persons suspected of having committed an offence under the Act.

The most important offences dealt with by the police are possession, possession with intent to supply to another, supply and production of controlled drugs.

The Misuse of Drugs Regulations 1985 lay down who is allowed to possess and supply controlled drugs whilst acting in their professional capacity e.g. medical practitioners, pharmacists, etc. and the manner in which they must do it. Requirements relating to prescriptions, the need for the prescriber to hand write the prescription in certain cases, dispensing by instalments, the safe custody of drugs and keeping records, etc. are all detailed. In addition the requirements relating to importation, exportation, production, supply and possession of controlled drugs are also defined.

The Regulations divide controlled drugs into five schedules and the level of supervision and control ranges from virtually total prohibition of availability and use in Schedule 1 to almost complete exemption of the requirements in Schedule 5.

- **SCHEDULE 1** – Drugs include raw opium, LSD and cannabis. Possession and supply, even by a doctor, are prohibited other than by Home Office licence. This is granted for educational and research purposes only.
- **SCHEDULE 2** – Drugs include heroin, morphine, pethidine, quinalbarbitone, amphetamine and cocaine. Home Office licences are required for import, export, production, supply and possession.
- **SCHEDULE 3** – Drugs include the barbiturates (excluding quinalbarbitone), buprenorphine, diethylpropion, mazindol and phentermine. A Home Office licence is required for importation and exportation, and authority required for production, possession and supply.
- **SCHEDULE 4** – Drugs include the benzodiazepines and pemoline. No licence is required to import or export these drugs and no authority required to possess them providing they are contained in the form of a medicinal product. Authority is required for their production and supply.
- **SCHEDULE 5** – Includes a range of controlled drugs, combined or compounded with other substances, in a preparation up to a stipulated maximum. Many of the preparations produced within the specifications of schedule 5 can be obtained over the counter

in a pharmacy. They consist of various remedies including those to suppress coughs, relieve mild pain and diarrhoea.

Because they contain such a low concentration of the drug, they are exempt from virtually all controlled drug requirements. No authority is required to possess them, but it is needed for their production and supply.

As the various types of drugs are described in this book, the effect of the Misuse of Drugs Regulations on them will be explained.

DEALING WITH A DRUG OFFENDER

A person who commits an offence against the Misuse of Drugs Act may be dealt with in a number of ways. If the offence is not considered to be serious (i.e. possession of a small quantity of cannabis for one's own use), and particularly if it is a first offence, the police may caution the individual.

This is a formal acknowledgement that the person has committed an offence and is usually accompanied by a strict warning regarding future behaviour. A caution is not a conviction but details of the incident may be brought to the attention of a court in any future proceedings. In addition, details may also be disclosed to future employers if the person later applies for particular types of jobs.

If the person has been previously cautioned for a similar offence or if the police consider a caution inappropriate he may have to appear before a Magistrates' Court where the offence is dealt with summarily. The responsibility for conducting the prosecution falls on the Crown Prosecution Service. On conviction he could be fined, although a suspended or short prison sentence are also possible.

More serious offences including supplying, possessing with intent to supply or illegally bringing the drugs into the country would probably be dealt with on indictment. This means the offence would be tried before a judge and jury at a higher criminal court or Crown Court. On conviction, severe penalties could be imposed.

The maximum penalties at the two levels of jurisdiction for possession and supply are:

Drug classification	Summary or indictable	Penalty
Possession		
Class A	Summary	6 months/£2000 or both
	Indictable	7 years/Fine or both
Class B	Summary	3 months/£500 or both
	Indictable	5 years/Fine or both
Class C	Summary	3 months/£200 or both
	Indictable	2 years/Fine or both
Supplying		
Class A	Summary	6 months/£2000 or both
	Indictable	Life imprisonment/Fine or both
Class B	Summary	6 months/£2000 or both
	Indictable	14 years/Fine or both
Class C	Summary	3 months/£500 or both
	Indictable	5 years/Fine or both

In addition, parole for drug offenders sentenced to more than five years' imprisonment has been severely restricted.

OFFENCES COMMITTED INSIDE PREMISES

It is illegal for an occupier or person in charge of any premises to allow anyone to produce, supply or offer to supply controlled drugs to another person. 'Supply' covers both selling and giving the drugs away. This offence includes permitting cannabis and opium to be smoked on the premises.

It is important for parents to take effective action if they know that their son or daughter is using or sharing drugs with friends in their house, as they may also be prosecuted for allowing it to happen. Employers will also commit the offence if they knowingly permit these activities to occur in the workplace. This responsibility extends to any person concerned in the management of the premises. Employers must take immediate action when it is known that illicit drugs are present in any part of the working environment.

The law allows a person (parent or employer) to take possession of the drugs to prevent another person from committing an offence, but they should immediately hand the drugs over to the police, or to someone lawfully entitled to receive them. Alternatively they should ensure that the drugs are immediately destroyed.

INVESTIGATION OF DRUG MONEY

The Drug Trafficking Offences Act 1986 was introduced to take the profit element out of drug trafficking. It gave the police and Customs new powers to investigate a person's financial affairs when they suspected an individual of being involved in drug trafficking. An order or warrant may be obtained requiring disclosure of information from records held by banks, other financial institutions and Government departments. A 'freezing' order may also be obtained to prevent assets being disposed of where proceedings have, or are about to be, started.

On conviction of a drug trafficking offence the Crown Court is required to impose a confiscation order on those people who have benefitted from drug trafficking. In 1989, 800 offenders were ordered to pay confiscation orders with a total value of £7.8 million. If the confiscation order is not paid in full, an additional period of imprisonment could be imposed. This is calculated by means of a sliding scale leading to a maximum of 10 years' imprisonment in default of a sum exceeding £1 million.

It is also a serious offence to assist a drug trafficker to 'launder' the proceeds of his drug trafficking and, in certain circumstances, to 'tip off' a drug trafficking suspect that he is being investigated. (The terms 'Drug Trafficking' and 'Drug Trafficking Offence' have special meanings which are defined in the Act.)

A large quantity of money, the proceeds of drug trafficking, is being counted by police officers. Such seizures are becoming commonplace
Photograph courtesy of: Cassidy and Leigh

In 1991 the Criminal Justice (International Co-operation) Act gave additional powers to Customs officers to seize cash from travellers if it was suspected to be connected with drug trafficking. The money can be held for up to two years, subject to magistrates' authority while investigations into its origins are carried out. If satisfied that the money is connected with drug trafficking, the court is empowered to forfeit sums of £10,000 and above.

SUPPLYING DRUG MISUSE ARTICLES

A recent amendment to the Misuse of Drugs Act made it an offence to supply or offer to supply articles used in the administration or preparation for administration of a controlled drug. This would include specially made pipes and drug administration kits which were being sold openly in certain shops. Hypodermic syringes are specifically exempt.

PAY PARTIES

In an effort to deter the organisers of acid house or pay parties, substantial increases in penalties for offences against the entertainment laws were made in 1990. Magistrates can now impose fines of up to £20,000 and/or six months' imprisonment for organising unlicensed entertainment or, if licensed, failing to comply with any condition of the licence e.g. exceeding the maximum number of persons permitted to attend.

In addition magistrates also have the power to order the confiscation of the proceeds of such events from persons convicted where they exceed £10,000.

THE MEDICINES ACT 1968

This controls the way medicines are made and supplied. Many controlled drugs are available as medicinal products. The Act divides them into prescription-only medicines; pharmacy medicines; and those medicines listed on the general sales list.

Prescription-only medicines can be supplied legally only on a doctor's prescription. These and pharmacy medicines must be sold or supplied at a registered pharmacy and under the supervision of a pharmacist.

Supermarkets and similar stores not registered as pharmacies can sell some of the least harmful medicinal products from the general sales list in small quantities.

OTHER SUBSTANCES

Tobacco, alcohol, glue and other solvents are legally available for non-medical use, though tobacco should not be sold to children under 16, nor alcohol to those under 18.

It is prohibited to supply people under 18 with substances which cause intoxication if inhaled, when the supplier knows or has cause to believe the substance is likely to be used for intoxication. (The Intoxicating Substances [Supply] Act 1985.)

It is also an offence to drive, attempt to drive or be in charge of a motor vehicle while unfit through drink or drugs. (Road Traffic Act 1972.)

IMPLICATIONS OF THE LAW IN THE WORKPLACE

This section is not meant to be a comprehensive statement of the law. It is a complicated subject involving both civil and criminal law and more detailed legal advice should be sought relating to specific circumstances.

The Health and Safety at Work Act 1974 places clear responsibilities on both employers and employees. Employers are required to ensure, as far as reasonably practicable, the health, safety and welfare of all their employees whilst at work. Employees must also take reasonable care of the health and safety of themselves and their fellow employees.

Drug abusers may put both their working colleagues and the public in danger by driving motor vehicles or other conveyances carelessly or negligently; by failing to operate powered machinery in a proper and safe manner; or by producing faulty goods.

If the employer allows a drug user (illicit user or person in treatment) to remain at a post where danger is caused to himself or others, the employer is not fulfilling his obligations under the Act. Third party employees injured as a result would also have a civil remedy for damages against the employer.

In the case of injury or other damage to a member of the public, action in civil law for compensation against the employee, or employer who may be vicariously liable, would also be a likely consequence.

Misuse of drugs in the workplace, therefore, may result in a number of adverse consequences for the employer. Although he may be successful in preventing drug activities occurring on his premises, dealing with individuals who misuse drugs in their own time and who may still be under their effects when they arrive at work is more difficult.

TRAVELLING ABROAD

Anyone travelling abroad must take care that they do not unwittingly either export from or import into the UK any prohibited drugs. This applies particularly to those on business, whether employers or their employees. Simple precautions include packing one's own suitcases, keeping them locked and not leaving them unattended before departure; not transporting any unopened gifts; and not accepting letters or packages abroad to be delivered or posted in the UK without actually seeing the contents. Travellers should always know exactly what is in their possession – in suitcases, hand luggage or in pockets.

Advice should also be sought before prescribed medicines are taken abroad. Just because they are lawfully prescribed in this country does not always mean that they can be taken out of the country or be in one's possession in another country.

Medical preparations that come within Schedules 4 and 5 of the Misuse of Drugs Regulations 1985 are not subject to an import or export licence. People who are prescribed drugs listed in Schedules 2 and 3 may only take around 15 days' supply abroad without a licence. The maximum quantity permitted varies according to the preparation. If particularly high doses are prescribed or if the prescription is for a period exceeding 15 days, an import or export licence may be required. Further information may be obtained from the Home Office Drugs Branch, Queen Anne's Gate, London, SW1 9AT.

The licence is only relevant to UK law and does not authorise entry or possession in the country to be visited. Enquiries should be made of the relevant Embassy or High Commission regarding necessary clearance.

THE
DRUGS

ANALGESICS

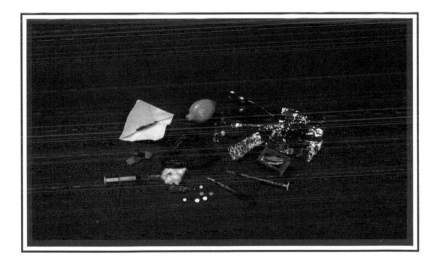

ANALGESICS

GENERAL DESCRIPTION

Analgesics are drugs which relieve pain and are produced either from the natural source of the opium poppy or synthetically.

Those derived from the opium poppy are known as **opiates** and are extremely potent. They include opium, morphine and heroin, and are frequently abused, particularly heroin. Opiates are so powerful that continuous use will almost certainly cause addiction. Even under medical supervision, patients have formed a physical dependence.

Users can become so dependent on the drug, both mentally and physically, that their whole life revolves around how, when and where to get the next 'fix'. They know that, without this, the deteriorating mental and physical spiral of withdrawal symptoms will start to take effect.

The medical profession uses opiates to relieve extreme pain from serious injury, disease or terminal illness. Secondary to this pain-killing function, the depressant effect of opiates on the central nervous system causes drowsiness and may even produce sleep.

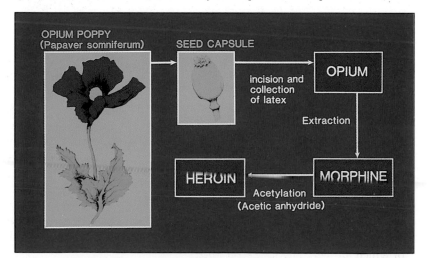

Opiates are also found in preparations to relieve mild pain such as headaches, coughing and stomach disorders such as diarrhoea and dysentery. Many of these preparations can be purchased over the counter in a pharmacy and are exempt from almost all the 'controlled drugs' legal provision by virtue of strength and dose. However, it is unlawful for the preparation to be supplied to another or possessed with intent to supply for non-medical purposes.

Synthetic analgesics, or **opioids**, have similar pain-killing qualities to the opiates. Manufactured for pharmaceutical use, they too may be misused at street level and can result in addiction – though some, like methadone, are given as a substitute when treating heroin addiction.

THE OPIATES

OPIUM

HISTORY Opium has been known for over 6,000 years. The use of opium was described by writers such as Coleridge and De Quincey, and as the medicine laudanum it was openly available until the twentieth century. While opium continues to be smoked and eaten in its countries of origin, notably in Asia, its impact in the West has recently been most serious in its refined forms as morphine and heroin.

SOURCE Opium is a natural product of the opium poppy (*Papaver Somniferum*), which grows in many countries, including Afghanistan, Pakistan, India, Cyprus, Iran, Burma, Laos, Thailand, China, Greece, Mexico, Poland, Lebanon and Indonesia.

The climatic conditions in the United Kingdom are not conducive to producing high-yield crops of opium poppies. A number of attempts have been made, including for culinary purposes, and the photograph overleaf shows part of a recent illicit crop grown in the west country.

Below the petals of the poppy flower is a sac or seed pod which produces a juice for a short time during the flowering period. This juice, rather like gum latex, is extracted by cutting a series of vertical or horizontal slits in the skin of the sac soon after the petals have dropped. From the cuts, a thick white juice oozes, quickly coagulates and turns brown.

The opium gum is collected, often with a crescent-shaped scraper, and rolled into balls. This is raw opium with a characteristic odour which is strong and pungent. It contains morphine and codeine, both of which are very effective pain-killers.

This crop of opium poppies is growing in the Bekaa Valley in the Lebanon

Opium poppies growing in the UK. The vertical cuts and opium gum can be seen on the poppy heads

Instances are occurring in this country where the poppy heads themselves are being boiled in water to produce a drink which is a weak solution of morphine. This activity may constitute an offence of producing a controlled drug.

RAW OPIUM Opium raw from the poppy is smoked, eaten or drunk as an infusion, particularly in its countries of origin, though in the United Kingdom such use is unlikely.

The freshness of the opium can be judged by its pliability – newly harvested it has the consistency of putty, but as it matures it becomes dry and hard. Raw opium is illegal. If found in the United Kingdom, it is almost certainly intended for refining, either into prepared opium, morphine or heroin. Such cases are extremely rare.

PREPARED OPIUM Raw opium is prepared for smoking simply by mixing it with water, then heating and filtering it to remove the impurities. It is further heated to obtain the required consistency. When fresh it is like black treacle, but as it matures it becomes firm like putty, and eventually as hard as a lump of coal.

Opium-smoking is legal in some countries, notably in the Middle East, where it is supplied as brown sticks about the size of a medium cigar.

HOW OPIUM IS TAKEN Opium is usually smoked. A simple method is called 'chasing the dragon'. A small piece of opium is placed on the inside of a roll of tinfoil, similar in size to the cardboard insert of a toilet roll. A match is run backwards and forwards on the outside of the tinfoil, and the fumes given off are inhaled.

The more sophisticated opium smoker may use a pipe specially made for the purpose. The pipe has a long thick stem with a bowl on one end. A small piece of opium, known as an opium 'pellet', is put in the bowl and heated, and the smoke is inhaled.

The sediment or 'dross' left in the smoking implements can contain up to 8 per cent morphine and this is subject to the full legal regulations.

LAWFUL OPIUM A very small amount of opium is used medicinally today, for example as an analgesic for patients suffering from cancer of the stomach.

It may occasionally be found at community pharmacies as a dark brown liquid tincture, or a brown powder for the manufacture of the tincture.

EFFECTS At first, the opium user may feel stimulated with enhanced imagination and speech. However, this is short-lived, as the respiration slows down, the imagination clouds, and the thinking processes become confused. This leads into a deep sleep and sometimes a coma.

DEPENDENCE As tolerance builds, larger doses of opium are needed to experience the same enjoyable sensations. However, the larger the dose, the quicker the deep sleep.

The seed pod of the opium poppy from which opium is obtained

To obtain opium, the seed pods are scored. A white juice oozes from the cuts, and quickly hardens and turns brown. This is raw opium. It is prepared for use by being mixed with water, heated and filtered

Prepared opium is sometimes further refined into sticks for smoking

Opium may be rolled into pellets like these before being smoked

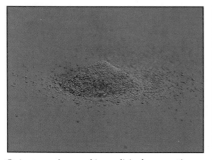

Opium powder, used in medicinal preparations

The sediment or 'dross' left after smoking opium. It may still contain enough of the drug to be a controlled substance

Long-term users show a noticeable deterioration in both their mental and physical capacities and reactions. Appetite is lost, and the body wastes. Body fluids dry up, blood pressure drops and the user feels permanently cold. Stomach pains, severe constipation and bladder disorders become frequent, and interest in personal relationships fades as the sexual drive diminishes. These are all signs of physical and psychological dependence, with other symptoms similar to those for morphine.

THE CURRENT SITUATION Opium abuse is not a significant problem in this country. The drug is only sporadically available, and while the occasional user may experience enjoyable fantasies, most merely become drowsy.

Nevertheless, it is against the law, not just to consume opium, but also to frequent a place used for its consumption or distribution. Further offences are possessing and supplying implements used in the preparation or smoking of opium, such as pots for boiling, pipes, prickers or contaminated tinfoil or matches.

Specially-made and highly decorative pipes used for smoking opium. The top pipe has a Chinese dragon engraved on it. The photo also shows a small metal box containing opium pellets

MORPHINE

HISTORY Morphine, the principal constituent of opium, was the first alkaloid to be isolated from a plant. It was discovered by a German pharmacist early in the nineteenth century.

Morphine is extracted by dispersing the raw opium in water then treating it with lime and filtering it. Ammonium chloride is added to the solution which results in the precipitation of crude morphine base. This is separated and further purified with other chemicals. The resulting substance is an analgesic three to five times stronger in its effect than opium itself.

MEDICAL USE Morphine is named after the Greek god of dreams, Morpheus. However, though it can encourage sleepiness, morphine is not a reliable hypnotic and is only used when the inability to sleep is due to pain. It is an important and powerful analgesic, particularly for treating persistent pain.

HOW MORPHINE IS TAKEN Morphine is administered medically by mouth, suppository and injection. As well as removing pain, it relaxes the patient and brings a happy feeling, which helps counteract the concern and apprehension that often accompany serious illness or operations.

Morphine's tendency to cause nausea has limited its popularity as a drug of abuse.

Morphine may be found in powder, tablet, liquid or ampoule form. Illicit users take the drug by swallowing tablets, drinking a liquid form, injecting it, heating and inhaling the vapour, or even as a suppository via the rectum.

RECOGNITION Pharmaceutical *morphine powder* is white and odourless and is used mainly in the preparation of liquids. The *liquids* themselves are not commonly encountered. They may be prescribed in linctus form as a cough suppressant, or in oral solutions of morphine hydrochloride which are used in the treatment of severe pain in terminal care.

Sometimes pharmaceutical morphine is stolen from community pharmacies. But it is not widely used by addicts because of its side-effects such as nausea and sickness.

Tableted pharmaceuticals containing morphine sulphate are produced under the brand name Sevredol and appear in two strengths: a 10mg blue capsule-shaped scored tablet; and a 20mg pink capsule-shaped scored tablet. Both are marked with 'IR' and the strength.

They are also produced in slow release form in various strengths

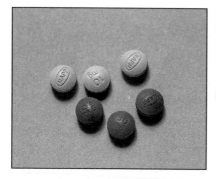

MST Continus morphine sulphate tablets showing 10mg (brown) and 30mg (purple). The 60mg, 100mg and 200mg strengths are of the same size tablets

Actual size of MST Continus morphine sulphate tablet

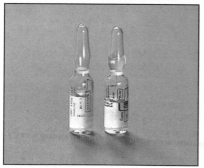

Morphine ampoules containing medicinal morphine in liquid form and ready for injection. They come in strengths of 10, 15 and 30mg

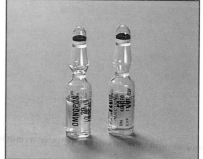

Omnopon ampoules containing the drug papaveretum — a mixture of opium alkaloids — in liquid form for injection. They are often carried in first aid kits on lifeboats and aircraft

under the MST Continus brand name. These are marketed as brown tablets (10mg dose); purple tablets (30mg); orange tablets (60mg); grey tablets (100mg) and green tablets (200mg). All are marked with the strength and 'NAPP'.

Other preparations that contain morphine include **injections** and **suppositories**. The sulphate is present in injections of various strengths (10, 15 and 30mg/ml), in 1 and 2ml ampoules, and in suppositories (15 and 30mg). The tartrate is present in injections of 10 and 15mg strengths, each with 50mg/ml of cyclizine tartrate in 1ml ampoules. They are produced under the brand name Cyclimorph.

Morphine is also contained in other medically prescribed substances including papaveretum injection and papaveretum and hyoscine injection. These preparations are produced under the brand name Omnopon: Omnopon 1ml ampoules – papaveretum 10 and 20mg/ml; and Omnopon and Scopolomine 1ml ampoules – papaveretum 20mg/ml. (Papaveretum consists of a mixture of the opium alkaloids and contains the equivalent of about 50 per cent anhydrous morphine.)

Morphine is also contained in the proprietary preparation Nepenthe (anhydrous morphine 8.4mg/ml), a brown-coloured oral solution.

Illicit morphine base has been found compressed into blocks. The blocks are made by treating the morphine base with hydrochloric acid to form a water-soluble salt which is cleaned by mixing with charcoal powder. After separation, the damp morphine hydrochloride powder is placed in a mould, pressed and dried.

The usual block size is 5×10×13cm, weighing about 1.3 kilograms.

Morphine powder ranges in colour from off-white to dark brown. It is rarely found at street level

Morphine granules, another form of illicit morphine. They are not common in this country

The colour may be anything from off-white to dark brown, and the trade mark '999' is commonly moulded onto the block.

Illegal morphine is also encountered in powder or granule form, in similar colours to the blocks. Abuse of morphine in these forms at street level is not common.

DEPENDENCE Dependence of the morphine type, as described below, is also applicable to other analgesic drugs in this section. It results from the continual use of morphine, or of drugs with morphine-type effects.

The euphoria produced by taking morphine can quickly develop into an overwhelming urge to continue its use. An increasing tolerance and then physical and psychological dependence on the drug can rapidly result.

Side-effects include nausea with occasional vomiting, constipation, confusion and sweating. This is sometimes accompanied by fainting, palpitations, sedation, restlessness and mood changes, dry mouth and high facial colour.

An overdose of morphine is likely to cause respiratory depression and low blood pressure. Coma and an overall physical decline, even death, may follow.

If a person addicted to morphine is denied a regular supply, withdrawal symptoms begin within a few hours, peak after 36 to 72 hours and then gradually fade. Withdrawal varies according to the individual and the degree of dependence. For some people it is like a mild bout of influenza; for others it can prove extremely traumatic and serious.

Common signs of withdrawal include irritability, anxiety, yawning, sneezing, headache, weakness, restlessness, sweating, insomnia, nausea, vomiting, muscle tremor, abdominal and muscle pain and cramps, increases in heart and respiratory rate and blood pressure.

CODEINE

Like morphine, codeine is an alkaloid naturally present in opium. It is found either as odourless, colourless crystals, or a white crystalline powder. The origin of its name is the Greek word meaning 'poppy head'.

Codeine is a pain-killer similar to morphine, but much less potent and with only mild sedative effects. It is either swallowed as tablets or a linctus for cough relief, or injected.

Codeine is useful for the relief of moderate pain as it is much less liable than morphine to cause dependence or toxic effects. If addiction does occur, through prolonged use of high doses, withdrawal is also less severe.

Side-effects from codeine include constipation, nausea, vomiting, dizziness and drowsiness. Non-medical doses produce restlessness, excitement and exhilaration. In children, codeine can cause convulsions.

HEROIN

HISTORY The discovery of morphine prompted the search for a new drug, with similar pain-killing qualities but without morphine's potential for addiction. Heroin, or diamorphine, was thought to be that drug.

It was first produced by a German company at the end of the nineteenth century by treating morphine with an acetylating substance (acetic anhydride is currently the chemical most commonly used for this purpose). Further chemicals are added to purify the mixture and, by filtering and precipitation, heroin is produced. Its name comes from the German word *heroisch*, meaning powerful or heroic.

Heroin is the strongest analgesic known, five to eight times more powerful than morphine. At first it was thought that heroin was non-addictive and could be used to relieve the symptoms of withdrawal from morphine. But it soon became clear that heroin was in fact much more addictive.

While heroin's therapeutic value is considerable, the dramatic spread of its abuse in recent years is a major and sinister problem

MEDICAL USE Heroin is extensively used in medicine in the UK, although its use in most other countries is strictly prohibited. No other analgesic is as strong or as effective. It relieves pain more quickly than morphine using a far smaller dose, though the effects wear off more quickly. As such it is used for accidents and injuries, and illnesses such as heart disease.

The main medicinal use of heroin is for the relief of pain from malignant diseases like cancer, when it is often administered in a mixture, particularly with cocaine.

Initial treatment brings the patient instant relief. But even under medical supervision, the body builds up a natural tolerance and the need for increasing doses may lead to addiction.

RECOGNITION Pharmaceutical or medicinal heroin (diamorphine) appears as:

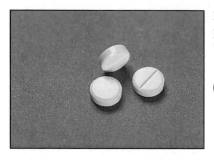

Heroin tablets. Unlike the heroin tablets produced in the past, these are intended for oral use, not for injection

Actual size of 10mg heroin tablet

Pharmaceutical heroin powder. Pure white and highly refined, it is used in various medicinal preparations

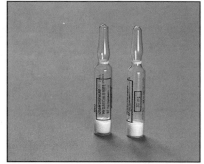

Freeze-dried heroin ampoules which are made in various strengths

POWDER – A white powder which is bitter to taste and used mainly for the manufacture of various forms of linctus.

TABLETS – These are manufactured as small white tablets containing 10mg of diamorphine hydrochloride.

AMPOULES – Heroin in ampoule form is not in fact a liquid. Heroin dissolved in sterilised water only remains good for about three weeks, before reverting back to morphine, so it is 'freeze dried' and then sealed into the glass phial.

These ampoules are found in different strengths between 5 and 500mg of diamorphine hydrochloride powder for reconstitution.

LIQUIDS – Heroin may be found as diamorphine linctus or, more commonly, as a specially prepared analgesic mixture.

Most of the heroin misused is not from medical supplies but has been smuggled into the country from abroad.

ILLICIT HEROIN The main sources of illicit heroin are Pakistan, Afghanistan, India, the Far East, Iran and Turkey. It is usually a powder, coloured from off-white to mid-brown.

Pakistan and Afghanistan heroin. Most heroin seized in this country today originates from the north-west frontier region of Pakistan and Afghanistan

In the last 25 years, there have been successive waves of Chinese and Iranian heroin, and now heroin from the Indian Sub-continent. Most of the heroin seized at present comes from Pakistan and Afghanistan in the form of heroin base, which is intended for smoking.

The distinctive Chinese heroin 'No 3' originates in the 'Golden Triangle' of Laos, Thailand and Burma and is probably distributed through Hong Kong or Singapore. It consists of small dirty grey or brown granules which resemble cat litter or Fisons Growmore. Produced mainly for smoking, it caused many problems in the early 1970s when injected by some British users. A more refined form of heroin from the same area is Chinese heroin 'No 4', a light, fluffy powder that may be white, off-white or even pink.

Chinese heroin 'No 3' in distinctive granules. Produced for smoking, it was encountered in London during the early 1970s

Chinese heroin 'No 4' – a more refined form of heroin originating in the same 'Golden Triangle' area as Chinese heroin 'No 3'

Recent seizures have been in the form of heavily compressed white powder blocks each measuring 12×8×2cm and weighing approximately 350mg. These are double or triple wrapped in clear plastic bearing a red trade mark of Chinese-style lions. The heroin, intended for injection, is 85–90 per cent pure.

This distinctive trademark appears on the plastic wrapping of the compressed Chinese heroin 'No 4' blocks

While little Chinese heroin is currently seized in the United Kingdom compared to that from the Indian Sub-continent, Europe is increasingly becoming an attractive target for the source countries. Chinese heroin could quickly re-emerge as traffickers attempt to take over part of the established market.

All heroin bought on the street is of unknown purity to the user. It can contain from below 10 per cent to as much as 95 per cent diamorphine. During 1990 the average purity of police heroin seizures was just under 40 per cent which is considered relatively high at street level.

Generally it is impure and contains a variety of substances. Some of these come from opium and some from the production process. Others which have included drugs such as phenobarbitone (see page 59),

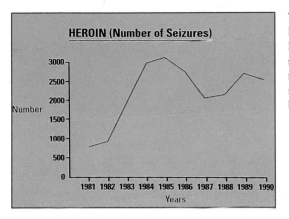

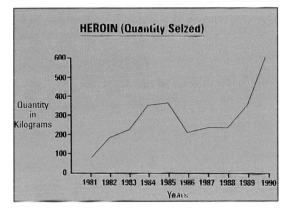

The two graphs clearly show how the illicit heroin situation has deteriorated in the UK since 1981 with an increasing number of annual seizures and massive quantities of heroin being recovered

methaqualone (a hypnotic and sedative), paracetamol (a non-opioid analgesic) and caffeine are added after manufacture but before importation. The type of drug added may indicate the source country of the heroin.

There are also suggestions that heroin is 'cut' (bulked out) at street level to increase profit. Diluents which are reported to have been used include glucose, sucrose, lactose, mannitol, curry powder, gravy mix and powdered soups, flour, baking powder, ephedrine (see page 91), or even abrasive cleaning powder, talc, plaster and brick dust – anything that will mix readily with the drug.

Note   Under no circumstances should heroin powder, or any other suspect substance, be tasted in an attempt to identify it. This practice, depicted on the television and in films, is totally wrong and can be dangerous. Only laboratory analysis or proper 'field tests' are acceptable drug identification methods.

HOW HEROIN IS TAKEN Present trends indicate that the majority of heroin addicts notified to the Home Office inject the drug. They may start by 'skin popping', an injection just below the skin's surface. Subsequently the heroin may be injected directly into a vein, which is known as 'mainlining'. 'Mainlining' is more difficult and often addicts rely on others for assistance. By this method the effects are felt almost immediately as the drug is carried through the bloodstream directly to the brain.

Heroin tablets or powder are mixed with a small quantity of water and heated. Lemon juice, citric acid or vitamin C may have to be added before the heroin will readily dissolve. Although conditions should be sterile, a teaspoon, match and water from the tap are commonly used.

A hypodermic syringe, or a medicine dropper with a hypodermic needle attached, is used to inject the liquid. Often a small loose ball of cotton wool is inserted into the bottom of the syringe or dropper to filter out undissolved powder and impurities as the solution is drawn into the equipment (called a 'works' or 'kit').

A tourniquet may be tied to make the veins swell up and easier to find. The liquid is then injected. After regular use the veins in the arms can become broken down, and addicts may then inject into their hands, legs and feet. Women sometimes inject into the breast.

The smoking of heroin was once restricted mainly to Chinese, Arab and Asian users in this country. In recent years it has become popular among experimenters, especially young first-time users who may be scared of the needle but willing to try a smoke.

Heroin can simply be smoked with tobacco in a hand-rolled ciga-rette. Much more common is 'chasing the dragon', when the heroin is placed on a piece of tinfoil and heated from beneath by means of a match, candle or cigarette lighter. The wisps of smoke which curl off are inhaled through a drinking straw or rolled tinfoil. The name derives from Hong Kong underworld slang to describe the undulating fumes, shaped like a dragon's tail.

A slight variation, using a matchbox cover instead of a straw or tinfoil, is known as 'playing the mouth-organ'.

Heroin can also be taken by sniffing it into the nostrils like snuff. This is popularly called 'snorting'. The drug is absorbed through the mucous membranes of the nose into the bloodstream, which carries it to the brain.

EFFECTS Initially the user experiences a sleepy, pleasant euphoria and total relief from all stress and anxiety. The enjoyable sensation or thrill, known as a 'buzz', consists of an overwhelming rush of pleasure as the drug enters the system.

Experimenters do not become addicted the first time they try heroin. But with regular use the body adjusts and tolerance sets in, until no pleasurable feelings are experienced at all. The body needs the drug just to stay more or less normal and to stave off the pains of withdrawal.

DANGERS Among the side-effects of taking heroin, the appetite is depressed and the body dehydrates. As a result, users tend not to eat properly and generally neglect themselves.

Heroin users rarely pay attention to hygiene. They may use dirty syringes, improvised equipment, share their syringes with others or mix the drug with impure water. In consequence, they suffer sores and ulcers and are vulnerable to many diseases. Death can result from septicaemia, hepatitis, jaundice, gangrene or pneumonia, as well as from an overdose. The risk of contracting HIV from shared and contaminated needles is a particular hazard.

There is an inherent danger in using street heroin as there is no way of knowing the purity level of the substance or what else has been added to increase the volume. Even strychnine has been found in samples analysed by the Metropolitan Police Forensic Science Laboratory.

Some addicts deliberately take heroin mixed with other drugs, particularly with cocaine as a 'speedball'. This is often done to prolong the cocaine 'high' since heroin allows the user to float down gently on a cloud of euphoria. The result, however, can be to accelerate dependence and cause a double addiction.

ADDICTION AND WITHDRAWAL Heroin addiction is both a physical and a psychological dependence. The withdrawal symptoms are similar to those of morphine but develop more quickly. Regardless of how it is taken, anyone regularly using heroin runs a high risk of forming a 'habit'. Then, as soon as the heroin in the system falls below a certain level, withdrawal begins.

Initially the user becomes restless and uneasy, and if there is no heroin or suitable substitute available may resort to bottles of cough mixture or patent medicines which contain mild opiates like codeine and can be purchased without prescription. Alcohol, barbiturates, benzodiazepines and amphetamine, sometimes in combination, may also be tried.

But the inevitable cycle continues. The user feels weak and irritable, the nose and eyes start to run, accompanied by yawning, trembling, sweating and uncontrollable sneezing. The limbs ache and pupils become dilated. While heart and respiratory rates, blood pressure and temperature all rise, an intense chill is felt, and the skin becomes covered in goose pimples – probably the origin of the term 'cold turkey'.

As withdrawal deepens, fever, stomach cramp and violent pains in the limbs develop. The body jerks involuntary through muscular spasms, and endures diarrhoea, sickness and constant pain.

Heroin withdrawal symptoms vary according to the individual and the degree of dependence. Some people experience the most devastating effects and others only mild discomfort. In its most serious form, withdrawal can continue for days before abating. Even when the physical symptoms seem to have disappeared, the system may still remain psychologically dependent on heroin, and the user may always be liable to return to the drug.

However hard the process, withdrawal symptoms can be overcome. Much depends on the desire and willpower of the individual, the support given by other people around, and staying free from the environment and lifestyle which precipitated the initial use of heroin.

OVERDOSING Overdosing on heroin is especially dangerous for beginners. The long-term user builds up tolerance and so can consume increasing quantities. However, a beginner taking the same amount would be in grave danger.

Even long-term addicts who have been deprived of the drug, perhaps by being in prison or hospital, and who return to their former quantity of heroin, may overdose because the body has lost its tolerance. Supplies which are purer than normal may cause overdoses in all users, new or experienced.

The symptoms of a heroin overdose are similar to those of morphine, although nausea and vomiting are less common.

RECOGNISING HEROIN ABUSE It is not possible to use the same site in a vein for repeated injections, and so the user works along a vein, puncturing, bruising and discolouring the surrounding area to produce clearly defined lines known as 'tracking marks'. These are tell-tale signs of a morphine or heroin abuser and are mainly visible on the arms or legs. Sores from infection also occur. Many new experimenters and users of heroin prefer to smoke or sniff it, rather than use injection, and so will not exhibit 'tracking marks'.

As well as syringes and needles, items which may suggest heroin use include: paper handkerchiefs or cotton wool (possibly blood-stained); spoons, matches, drinking straws and pieces of tinfoil; and

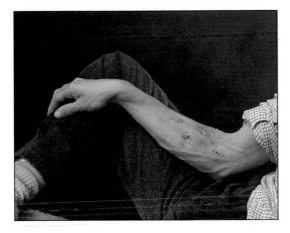

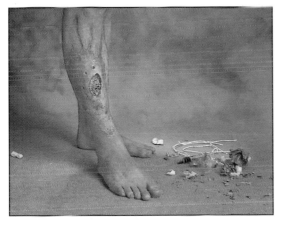

'Tracking marks', along the veins in the arm and leg. Ulcers, sores, puncture wounds and bruises develop at the site of repeated injections

A street user deal of heroin which may vary from 125—250mg and cost approximately £25

small squares of paper folded to form a secure envelope (known as 'wraps' or 'street deals') which can hold a small amount of powder.

Some users look neglected, behave aggressively and anti-socially, are unable to concentrate and become deceitful and convincing liars. However, there are also many users who display none of these outward signs. They may hold down a regular job and maintain an acceptable appearance, while continuing to satisfy their need, possibly from an illicit source, but more probably from a Drug Dependency Clinic.

SLANG NAMES At street level, heroin is known by a number of slang expressions, including:

			Horse
'H'	Scat	Chi	Junk
Smack	Chinese 'H'	Scag	Elephant
Stuff	Tiger	Harry	Dragon

THE OPIOIDS

PETHIDINE

MEDICAL USE Pethidine is an analgesic that is used medically instead of morphine, mostly in childbirth to reduce labour pains and before and after surgical operations. Although its effects are similar, they are not as powerful or prolonged.

Pethidine has local anaesthetic and mild sedative actions. It is not a strong hypnotic, and so is less effective than morphine when an individual is in continuous pain and unable to sleep as a result.

RECOGNITION The forms in which pethidine is produced are: a white powder; pethidine hydrochloride tablets – 50mg; and pethidine hydrochloride injections – 50 and 100mg (these are available in two concentrations – 10mg/ml and 50mg/ml).

Pethidine injections are also available under the brand name Pamergan P100. This consists of a mixture of 100 mg of pethidine hydrochloride and 50mg of promethazine hydrochloride in 2ml ampoules.

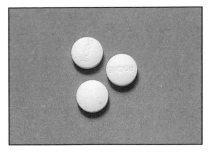

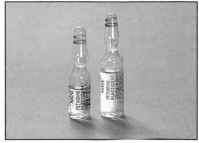

Pethidine tablets are often used in hospitals

 Actual size of 50mg pethidine tablet

Ampoules containing pethidine in injectable form. The variation in ampoule size indicates different strengths, i.e. 50 and 100mg

ABUSE The analgesic effect of pethidine is accompanied by mild euphoria. It has occasionally been abused, particularly by medical practitioners, nurses and others in the health professions.

DEPENDENCE Continuous administration of pethidine may lead to dependence of the morphine type, and addicts have been known to require doses of up to 4 grams a day. The effects do not last as long as morphine and withdrawal symptoms begin more quickly.

Side-effects include nausea, vomiting, palpitations, dizziness, headache, weakness and constipation. An overdose may cause tremors, involuntary muscular movements, dilated pupils and convulsions, sometimes followed by respiratory depression and coma.

METHADONE

Methadone is a powerful analgesic similar to morphine, but without such a strong sedative effect. In its basic form it is a white crystalline powder. Because it is closely associated with heroin and has comparable effects, methadone is widely abused.

USE IN TREATING HEROIN ADDICTION Methadone is widely prescribed by doctors in the treatment of heroin addiction. It counteracts heroin's euphoria and prevents the onset of heroin withdrawal. Because methadone's effects last longer than those of heroin, the frequency of administration is reduced to once or twice a day.

Methadone is initially given to addicts in daily doses comparable to their heroin 'habit' with the aim of slowly withdrawing the addict

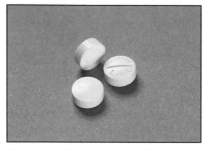

Physeptone tablets containing methadone, widely used in the treatment of heroin addiction

Physeptone ampoules, with methadone in injectable form

Actual size of Physeptone tablet

Methadone linctus contains methadone hydrochloride and may be prescribed to control a distressful cough in terminal disease

Methadone mixture (BNF), a greenish-coloured liquid is two-and-a-half times stronger than methadone linctus and it is used in the treatment of heroin addiction. It contains an irritant which discourages injecting

from illicit injectable heroin and on to reducing doses of oral methadone linctus.

Sometimes complete withdrawal of methadone is not possible, and a methadone maintenance dose may continue for months or even years.

RECOGNITION Methadone is available in various forms and strengths: a white powder; white physeptone tablets – 5mg; physeptone injections – 10mg/ml; methadone linctus of strength

2mg/5ml (brown liquid); and methadone mixture (BNF) of strength 1mg/ml (green liquid).

More recently methadone injections have been made available by special order in the following strengths: 50mg/ml; and 35mg/3.5ml; in chocolate-coloured ampoules.

DEPENDENCE Although regular use of methadone may lead to dependence, it is generally considered less serious than morphine or heroin dependence and easier to treat. The methadone addict is often able to lead a relatively normal life.

Among methadone's side-effects are light-headedness, dizziness, nausea and vomiting, a dry mouth and sweating. More severe symptoms include respiratory depression and low blood pressure. Circulatory failure and deepening coma may follow and deaths have resulted from respiratory failure.

DEXTROMORAMIDE

Dextromoramide is an analgesic used to treat moderate or severe pain.

Abuse by addicts is a continuing occurrence and can result in dependence similar to that of morphine. Overdosing on dextromoramide has comparable dangers and effects to those of methadone, sometimes with added unpleasant hallucinations.

Palfium tablets contain the drug dextromoramide. They are made in two strengths, 5mg (white) and 10mg (peach-coloured)

Actual size of both 5mg and 10mg Palfium tablets

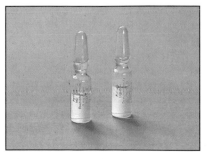

Palfium ampoules, with dextromoramide in injectable form

RECOGNITION Dextromoramide (as tartrate) is produced under the proprietary name of Palfium: a white scored tablet – 5mg; a peach-coloured scored tablet – 10mg; injections – 5 and 10mg/ml in 1ml ampoules; and suppositories – 10mg.

DANGERS – See Dipipanone below.

DIPIPANONE

Dipipanone is related to methadone and used medically in the treatment of moderate or severe pain. It was widely and increasingly abused by addicts in the past, and in 1984 was added to the list of drugs which can only be prescribed for the treatment of addiction by doctors licensed by the Home Office. Although addicts turned to more available drugs like dextromoramide and dihydrocodeine, misuse of dipipanone still occurs.

RECOGNITION Dipipanone is dispensed as a distinctive pink tablet under the name Diconal, containing 10mg of dipipanone hydrochloride and 30mg of cyclizine hydrochloride and coded 'WELLCOME F3A'.

Diconal, a distinctive pink-coloured tablet containing the drug dipipanone which was widely misused until the prescribing restrictions were tightened up. It was often dissolved in water and injected

Actual size of Diconal tablet

ABUSE Although the tablets are meant to be taken orally, addicts often crush and dissolve them in water for injection. This carries a particular risk of a serious fall in blood pressure. Continuous use of dipipanone may produce dependence of the morphine type, and the effect of an overdose is similar to that of methadone.

DANGERS Dipipanone tablets, like dextromoramide (page 49), are especially dangerous if dissolved in water and injected. As part of the tablet is a filler, it will not dissolve completely and may result in the veins becoming blocked. This can cause gangrene in the hands or feet and possibly lead to death.

DIHYDROCODEINE

Dihydrocodeine is used medically to relieve less severe pain, and as a cough suppressant.

RECOGNITION It is produced under its generic name in three forms of dihydrocodeine tartrate: tablets – 30mg; injections – 50mg/ml in 1ml ampoules; and an elixir – 10mg/5ml. Dihydrocodeine tartrate

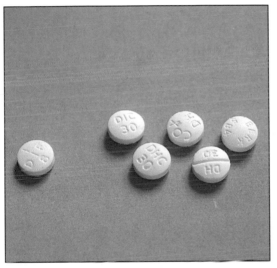

A DF 118 tablet is shown to the left of a selection of similar non-proprietary preparations produced by other manufacturers. They all contain the controlled drug dihydrocodeine, but because of the low concentration in the preparations, it is not an offence under the Misuse of Drugs Act to possess them

Actual size of DF 118 tablet

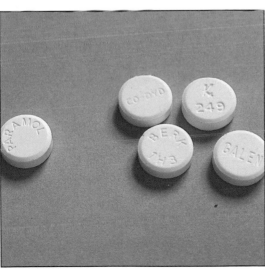

A selection of the compound preparation co-dydramol containing dihydrocodeine tartrate and paracetamol

Actual size of the brand name product Paramol

appears in the well-known proprietary brand DF 118. It is produced as a white 30mg tablet marked with the tablet name, as a 50mg/ml injection in 1ml ampoules and as an elixir containing 10mg/5ml in syrup.

Other manufacturers produce equivalent medical preparations, a sample of which is shown in the photograph on page 51, together with a DF 118 tablet for comparison purposes. At street level they may all be incorrectly referred to as 'DFs'.

Co-dydramol tablets contain dihydrocodeine tartrate 10mg and paracetamol 500mg. This preparation is described as a compound opiate analgesic.

CONTROLS Dihydrocodeine is a Class B drug and DF 118 tablets, together with the non-proprietary equivalents and co-dydramol can only be obtained on prescription. These preparations only contain a small quantity of the drug dihydrocodeine and are therefore excepted from the prohibition on importation, exportation and possession (i.e. Schedule 5 drugs). It is an offence, however, for an unauthorised person to supply these tablets, or possess them with intent to supply to another.

Dihydrocodeine in its injectable form is subject to the full control of the Misuse of Drugs Act.

The general lack of control, particularly in the past over DF 118 tablets, has made it difficult to monitor prescribing practices.

The misuse of dihydrocodeine increased following the introduction of prescribing restrictions on dipipanone and the difficulty in obtaining that drug. Dihydrocodeine may still be partially filling that vacuum.

DEPENDENCE The effects of dependence and overdosing are similar to those of morphine, though side-effects are usually less serious.

DANGERS A particular danger associated with abusing co-dydramol tablets, is that to ingest sufficient of the dihydrocodeine, a large over-dose of paracetamol will be taken. Paracetamol is highly dangerous in even modest overdose, and may result in fatal liver damage.

BUPRENORPHINE

Buprenorphine is used medically to relieve moderate to severe pain. Its effects last longer than morphine and it is an effective analgesic for eight to 12 hours.

DEPENDENCE Buprenorphine is thought to have a low dependence potential. Its side-effects are similar to those of morphine but less

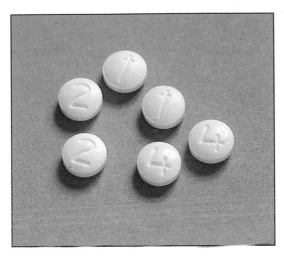

Temgesic tablets contain the drug buprenorphine. They come in two strengths, 200 and 400 micrograms

Actual size of Temgesic tablets

serious. Use of this drug may bring about withdrawal symptoms in individuals dependent on other opioids.

RECOGNITION Buprenorphine (as hydrochloride) appears both in tablet and ampoule form under the brand name Temgesic. The tablets are white and of two strengths: 200 microgram marked with 2; 400 microgram marked with 4. Both are marked with a symbol resembling a sword.

A Temgesic injection contains 300 microgram/ml of buprenorphine and is available in 1ml and 2ml ampoules.

ABUSE Temgesic is commonly attractive to misusers. However, there is little evidence that the drug in injectable form is widely misused. The reported method of administration is by crushing the tablets, dissolving and injecting – with all the dangers associated with that practice.

CONTROLS Buprenorphine is a Class C drug and it is an offence to possess, except when prescribed, possess with intent to supply and supply the drug to another.

DEXTROPROPOXYPHENE

In its basic form, dextropropoxyphene is a white or slightly yellow powder with a bitter taste. It is used medically as a mild analgesic, with properties similar to codeine.

RECOGNITION Dextropropoxyphene appears in a compound opiate

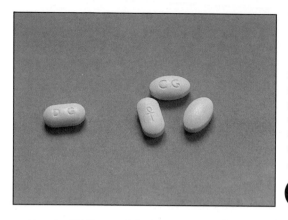

The Distalgesic tablet marked 'DG' is shown to the left of a selection of co-proxamol tablets produced by other manufacturers. Although they all contain the controlled drug dextropropoxyphene, because of the low concentration of the drug, it is not an offence under the Misuse of Drugs Act to possess them

Actual size of Distalgesic tablet

analgesic (32.5mg of dextropropoxyphene and 325mg of paracetamol) under the non-proprietary name of co-proxamol.

It is produced under the brand name Distalgesic in a white oblong tablet marked 'DG'.

Dextropropoxyphene also appears in other proprietary products, both on its own and mixed with other drugs.

CONTROLS Dextropropoxyphene is a Class C drug and can only be obtained on prescription. The small quantity of the drug contained in Distalgesic and the other non-proprietary co-proxamol products means that it is not an offence under the Misuse of Drugs Act to possess, export or import the drug in that form. It is an offence for an unauthorised person to supply them or be in possession with intent to supply to another person.

DEPENDENCE Continuous use of high doses may lead to morphine-type dependence. In overdose, convulsions can occur, especially when dextropropoxyphene is combined with a stimulant or similar drug.

ANALGESICS

Drugs	Class	Medical uses	Dependence potential Physical	Dependence potential Psychological	Tolerance	Duration of effect (in hours)	Methods of administration licit and illicit	Possible effects[1]	Possible effects of overdose[1]	Possible withdrawal symptoms	Medical preparation in which individual drugs occur[2]
Opium	A	Analgesic, pre-operative medication, anti-diarrhoeal, cough suppressant	High	High	Yes	3 to 6	Oral, injection, smoked	Euphoria, drowsiness, respiratory depression, constricted pupils, nausea	Slow and shallow breathing, clammy skin, convulsions, coma, possible death	Watery eyes, runny nose, yawning, loss of appetite, irritability, tremors, panic, chills and sweating, cramps, nausea	
Morphine	A	Analgesic	High	High	Yes	3 to 6	Oral, injection, smoked				Omnopon, Sevredol, MST Continus, Cyclimorph
Codeine	B	Analgesic, cough suppressant, anti-diarrhoeal	Moderate	Moderate	Yes	3 to 6	Oral, injection				
Diamorphine (Heroin)	A	Analgesic	High	High	Yes	3 to 6	Oral, injection, sniffed, smoked				
Pethidine	A	Analgesic	High	High	Yes	3 to 6	Oral, injection				Pethidine, Pamergan P100

Drugs	Class	Medical uses	Dependence potential — Physical	Dependence potential — Psychological	Tolerance	Duration of effect (in hours)	Methods of administration licit and illicit	Possible effects[1]	Possible effects of overdose[1]	Possible withdrawal symptoms	Medical preparation in which individual drugs occur[2]
Methadone	A	Analgesic, heroin substitute (in treatment of addiction)	High	High	Yes	12 to 24	Oral, injection	Euphoria, drowsiness, respiratory depression, constricted pupils, nausea	Slow and shallow breathing, clammy skin, convulsions, coma, possible death	Watery eyes, runny nose, yawning, loss of appetite, irritability, tremors, panic, chills and sweating, cramps, nausea	Physeptone
Dextromoramide	A	Analgesic	High	High	Yes	2 to 4	Oral, injection, suppository				Palfium
Dipipanone	A	Analgesic	High	High	Yes	4 to 6	Oral, injection				Diconal
Dihydrocodeine	B	Analgesic	High	High	Yes	3 to 6	Oral, injection				DF 118[3] Co-dydramol[3]
Buprenorphine	C	Analgesic	Mild	Mild	Yes	8 to 12	Oral, injection				Temgesic
Dextropropoxyphene	C	Mild analgesic	Mild	Mild	Yes	2 to 4	Oral				Co-proxamol[3] Distalgesic[3]

[1] The effects of individual drugs may be enhanced when taken with alcohol or in combination with other drugs.

[2] This list is not exhaustive. Some of these products are no longer supplied on the National Health Service. Generic equivalents may be prescribed and can differ in form, colour and manufacturer's markings, making visual identification more difficult.

[3] Because of the low concentration of drugs in non-proprietary dihydrocodeine preparations, DF 118, co-dydramol preparations and co-proxamol preparations including Distalgesic, it is not an offence to possess, import or export them. It is an offence to supply and possess with intent to supply without authority. They can only be obtained on prescription.

DEPRESSANTS

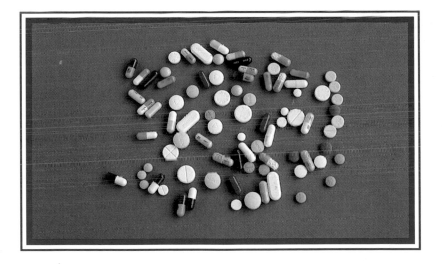

DEPRESSANTS

GENERAL DESCRIPTION

Depressants are drugs which, by depressing the central nervous system, will calm you down or send you to sleep. They are produced pharmaceutically in huge quantities and a wide range of forms, as barbiturate and benzodiazepine tranquillisers and hypnotics.

Hypnotics are those drugs which produce sleep. With continued or excessive use they can be very toxic and addictive, especially in barbiturate form. As they generally have no pain-killing action, they are given with an analgesic when pain is preventing sleep.

Depressants are widely prescribed to treat stress, anxiety, mental disorders and sleeplessness, and some are valuable in epilepsy cases. Medical use has itself produced a serious dependence problem, and they have been frequently misused at street level where they are known as 'sleepers' or 'downers'.

Many other substances have hypnotic or sedative effects, including alcohol and opiate analgesics, but there are particular problems associated with sleeping pills and tranquillisers which are so commonly available both legally and illegally.

It is important that anyone being treated with depressants ensures that they are stored safely away from children.

BARBITURATES

HISTORY Throughout history people have relied on all kinds of remedies to help them go to sleep. But there was no known synthetic substance to induce sleep until the discovery of barbituric acid on St Barbara's Day in 1899. Though not itself an hypnotic, this has since formed the basis for the development of hundreds of barbiturate and barbiturate-type drugs.

Only a few barbiturates were generally prescribed, among them Tuinal, Seconal and Amytal. Use of these, however, became widespread. It was thought that they had clear medical and psychological benefits but their potential for dependence increasingly became a matter of serious concern.

EFFECTS While all barbiturates depress the central nervous system, they can vary extensively in effect, duration and toxicity. Most have been used both as hypnotics and sedatives, depending on the reason for prescription and the amount taken.

Barbiturates are categorised according to how long their effects last. This depends not only on the drug, but also on the time the body takes to eliminate it through the kidneys and liver.

IDENTIFICATION Barbiturates come as tablets or capsules in various sizes and colours. Though the more common types are easy to identify, under illicit distribution the contents are not necessarily what the packaging suggests. For example, some capsules easily come apart and the powder inside may have been replaced by another substance. As with other drugs, only proper laboratory analysis provides safe identification.

VARIETIES

LONG-ACTING BARBITURATES – These produce several hours' sleep. They can quickly build up in the body, resulting in a 'hangover' which is dangerous when it impairs skills or spoils concentration. Such drugs are prescribed for nervous insomnia, some forms of epilepsy and mental disturbance, and to relieve migraine.

The effects of long-acting barbiturates start within an hour and last for up to 10 hours. The most common long acting barbiturate is phenobarbitone. Misuse is occasionally reported.

INTERMEDIATE-ACTING BARBITURATES – These work more quickly – their effects usually start within 15 to 30 minutes and they last from two to eight hours. They are less likely to produce a 'hangover' effect, and were prescribed for people who had difficulty going to sleep. They were also used to treat anxiety and convulsions, and as pre-operative sedatives.

Because of the inherent dangers with these drugs they are now mainly restricted to the treatment of severe intractable insomnia in patients already taking barbiturates. Likewise they are seldom used to treat anxiety.

The intermediate-acting barbiturates are most likely to be misused. They include:

Amylobarbitone which is contained in the drug Amytal. This is produced in the form of white tablets marked 'LILLY' and of various strengths: 30mg coded T56; 50mg coded T37; and 100mg coded T32.

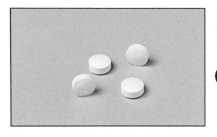

Amytal tablets contain the barbiturate drug amylobarbitone in various strengths. The tablets shown are 30mg

 Actual size of Amytal tablet

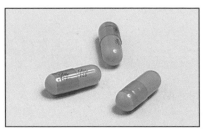

Sodium Amytal capsules contain amylobarbitone sodium. They come in two strengths (the one shown here is 60mg). Street names include 'birds' and 'blue heavens'

 Actual size of Sodium Amytal capsule

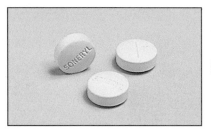

Soneryl tablets, with 100mg of the barbiturate drug butobarbitone

 Actual size of Soneryl tablet

Seconal Sodium capsules, containing the drug quinalbarbitone sodium, are produced in two strengths. The one shown is 50mg. They are known as 'reds' or 'red devils'

 Actual size of Seconal Sodium capsule

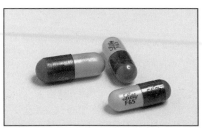

Tuinal capsules are distinctive orangey red and blue capsules, with the drugs quinalbarbitone sodium and amylobarbitone in equal parts. Street names include 'rainbows' and 'reds and blues'

 Actual size of Tuinal capsule

Amylobarbitone sodium, found under the brand name Sodium Amytal (often known just as 'Amytal'), comes in blue capsules of either 60mg or 200mg strength and is marked 'LILLY' F23 and F33 respectively. It also appears in a white 60mg tablet coded U43.

Butobarbitone appears in the drug Soneryl. It is a pink scored tablet of 100mg that is marked 'SONERYL'.

Quinalbarbitone sodium is the active constituent in Seconal Sodium, often simply called 'Seconal'. It is produced in orange capsules of two strengths, 50 and 100mg, both marked 'LILLY' and coded F42 and F40 respectively.

Quinalbarbitone sodium and amylobarbitone are two drugs that are contained in equal parts in orange and blue capsules marked with the proprietary name 'TUINAL' and F65.

VERY SHORT-ACTING BARBITURATES – These are used for intravenous injection in hospital. Almost immediately they produce complete anaesthesia, of short duration or before a general anaesthetic. They may also be used to control convulsions. Abuse is rare.

DEPENDENCE Barbiturates were freely prescribed by doctors particularly during the 1950s and 60s and their potential for dependence and abuse was not immediately appreciated. The dangers were eventually highlighted by the growing addiction problem and the large number of people who died from barbiturate overdose. In 1978 over 50 per cent of all drug-related deaths in London showed barbiturates as a cause of death.

The prescribing of barbiturates is now discouraged with benzodiazepines being, in most cases, the preferred alternative. However, use still occurs in all sectors of society and no-one knows exactly how many people still regularly use barbiturates to help them sleep or for other reasons.

The physical and psychological dependence which results from prolonged use can be even more serious than opiate addiction, with worse withdrawal symptoms.

ABUSE Because such large quantities have been legally distributed, many have found their way onto the black market. Availability at street level has decreased over the last few years but seizures are still being made by the police.

Dependence and tolerance are most likely with the intermediate-acting barbiturates.

Misusers feel relieved of fears, worry, tension and anxiety. They may react unpredictably, or show signs of mental confusion. Some are stimulated, feeling sociable, happy and relaxed. But to the real world they appear drunk – speech becomes slurred and they often lose their balance and so suffer accidental injury.

The effects are considerably increased when combined with alcohol or other drugs. Accidental fatal overdoses can occur from such mixing, when none of the drugs on its own is a serious danger. The most common type of suicide is taking sleeping tablets with alcohol.

Some users dissolve barbiturates in water and inject them into their veins. This is perhaps the most dangerous of all forms of drug abuse. Some of the powder remains undissolved, and particles lodge under the skin causing abscesses and sometimes gangrene.

Users of other drugs may also turn to barbiturates. Opiate addicts unable to obtain their usual supply take them to ward off withdrawal symptoms, and alcoholics trying to give up alcohol use them to counteract DTs (*delirium tremens*). They are also taken by amphetamine and LSD abusers to help calm them down from the effects of their primary drug.

ADDICTION AND WITHDRAWAL Prolonged use causes both physical and psychological dependence, and if the supply is suddenly stopped or even reduced there are serious withdrawal symptoms.

After initial anxiety and inability to relax or sleep, users start to tremble and their temperature and heart rate rise. There are feelings of faintness, nausea and dizziness, with involuntary muscle movements and abdominal cramp. There may be terrifying hallucinations and convulsions which can cause permanent brain damage. Without proper medical treatment, death may result.

OVERDOSE The quantity of barbiturates resulting in an overdose depends on the individual, the type of drug and what other drugs are taken at the same time. The margin of safety is very narrow and the severe toxic effects of the drug can easily lead to death – particularly in combination with alcohol.

The pulse grows weak and quick, pupils become dilated, respiration is shallow and the skin turns clammy. The user will sink into a coma and death may follow. Death can also result from inhalation of vomit, pneumonia or hypothermia if the user falls asleep in an exposed place.

CONTROLS Until 1985, barbiturates were simply classed as prescription-only medicines, so possession in itself was not an offence. Barbiturates are now listed as Class B drugs. This means that, while doctors can still prescribe them, it is illegal to possess, if they have not been prescribed for the user, possess with intent to supply or supply barbiturates.

SLANG NAMES

Barbiturates		Amytal	= Angels
general	= Barbs		Birds
	Candy		Blue heavens
	Goofballs		
	Sleeping pills	Seconal	= Reds
	Peanuts		Red birds
	Downers		Red devils
	Sleepers		Seggy
		Tuinal	= Rainbows
			Red and blues
			Double troubles

BENZODIAZEPINES – TRANQUILLISERS AND HYPNOTICS

HISTORY *Rauwolfia Serpentina* is an evergreen bush which grows in parts of Asia, with similar varieties in Central Africa and Central and South America. Its dried roots have been used for hundreds of years in the treatment of many ailments, including nervous disorders, blood pressure and insomnia.

The roots contain a number of alkaloids useful in medicine. Reserpine, one of the most important, was separated by Swiss chemists in the early 1950s and used as a tranquillising drug to treat high blood pressure and mental illness.

The chemical structure of reserpine was analysed and produced in synthetic form as drugs which have similar effects. Two main types have been developed; **major tranquillisers** which treat severe mental illness, and **minor tranquillisers** for less serious depression, anxiety and insomnia.

MEDICAL USE The **major tranquillisers**, including the group of drugs known as phenothiazines, are mainly used in cases of psychosis, such as schizophrenia, mania and senile dementia. They are also valuable in treating behavioural disorders in children. Major tranquillisers do not produce physical dependence even when taken over long periods.

The **minor tranquillisers** and **hypnotics** mainly come from a group of drugs known as benzodiazepines. The principal uses are: as anxiolytics (sedatives) or tranquillisers to treat restlessness, depression, tension and anxiety; as hypnotics or sleeping pills for the treatment of insomnia; as muscle relaxants; as anti-convulsants for treating certain types of epilepsy; as a pre-surgery sedative to relax patients before an operation; and to ease alcohol withdrawal symptoms.

Benzodiazepines are the most frequently used anxiolytics and hypnotics; barbiturates are no longer recommended.

Tranquillisers bring about a relaxed state in a patient without necessarily producing sleep. Most tranquillisers will induce sleep if given in large doses. Certain benzodiazepines are specifically prescribed as hypnotics but these will also sedate when given in lower doses during the day.

Since this group of drugs was introduced in 1960 it has become one of the most commonly prescribed drugs of any kind among all sections of the community. It is estimated that in 1988 almost 19 million prescriptions for benzodiazepines alone were issued by family doctors, the majority going to women.

VARIETIES AND RECOGNITION The benzodiazepines most often prescribed were at one time easily identifiable because they became known to the general public by their manufacturer's brand name. This has now changed and where generic equivalents are available, doctors are encouraged to prescribe them. This allows pharmacists to dispense any suitable product which might not necessarily be one of the better-known proprietary brands. The only exception to this is in cases where alternative preparations do not suit particular patients who need to continue with the same brand. In addition certain of these products are now no longer supplied at the expense of the National Health Service.

This change has made the visual identification of certain types of drugs, particularly benzodiazepines, much more difficult and less reliable. Photographs of the well-known brand name preparations are shown together with a sample of non-proprietary preparations.

There is no obligation on different manufacturers to produce identical looking products for the same medical preparation. Some look very similar, others are quite different. The accompanying photographs clearly show the difficulties and hence the inherent dangers in putting too much reliance on a visual identification.

TRANQUILLISERS

Tranquillisers can be divided into two groups: **intermediate-acting** and **long-acting**. Although there is a greater risk of withdrawal symptoms with the former there is more risk of drug accumulation, and therefore adverse effects in particularly susceptible individuals, by using long-acting tranquillisers.

Short-term (two to four weeks) minimal doses are recommended for the relief of anxiety that is severe, disabling or causing extreme distress. Use should be monitored and discontinued as soon as possible. Withdrawal should be gradual to prevent a return of the original symptoms. The benzodiazepines marketed as tranquillisers include:

LORAZEPAM (INTERMEDIATE-ACTING) – Lorazepam is produced as 1 and 2.5mg tablets in generic products. It also appears under the brand name Ativan in blue tablets of 1mg and yellow tablets of 2.5mg strength. Ativan tablets are oblong in shape, scored and marked A1 and A2.5 respectively. Ativan injections 4mg/ml in 1ml ampoules are also available.

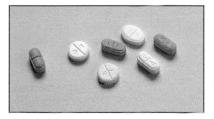

The blue 1mg Ativan tablet is shown to the left of a number of medicinal preparations produced by other manufacturers under the non-proprietary or generic title of lorazepam

 Actual size of 1mg Ativan tablet

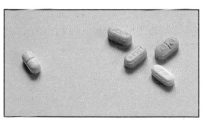

The yellow 2.5mg Ativan tablet is shown to the left of a sample of non-proprietary lorazepam preparations produced by other manufacturers

 Actual size of 2.5mg Ativan tablet

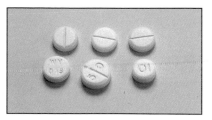

A sample of the medicinal preparations produced by manufacturers under the non-proprietary title oxazepam

OXAZEPAM (INTERMEDIATE-ACTING) – Oxazepam is produced in 10, 15 and 30mg tablets in generic products.

CHLORDIAZEPOXIDE (LONG-ACTING) – Chlordiazepoxide is produced as 5, 10 and 25mg tablets; and 5 and 10mg capsules in generic products. It is also contained in the brand name preparation Librium in green tablets of 5, 10 and 25mg strength, or in capsules coloured green and yellow (5mg) or green and black (10mg). All are marked 'LIB' and with their strength.

Librium tablets and capsules of 5mg strength. Librium contains the drug chlordiazepoxide

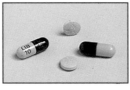

Librium tablets and capsules in a stronger concentration of 10mg

Librium tablets of 25mg strength. The green colour of the tablet darkens as the drug strength increases

 Actual size of 5mg Librium tablet

 Actual size of 10mg Librium tablet

 Actual size of 25mg Librium tablet

 Actual size of 5mg Librium capsule

 Actual size of 10mg Librium capsule

DIAZEPAM (LONG-ACTING) – Diazepam is produced in 2, 5 and 10mg tablets and as an elixir in generic products. It also appears under the brand name Valium. This comes in white tablets of 2mg strength; yellow tablets of 5mg strength; and blue tablets of 10mg strength. All Valium tablets are scored on one side and marked with the drug strength and the word 'ROCHE' on the other. Valium syrup, suppositories and injections are also available.

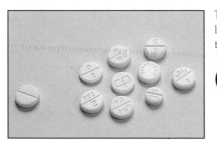

The white 2mg Valium tablet is shown to the left of a sample of non-proprietary products of the same strength

 Actual size of 2mg Valium tablet

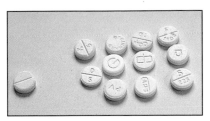

The yellow 5mg Valium tablet is shown to the left of a sample of non-proprietary products of the same strength

Actual size of 5mg Valium tablet

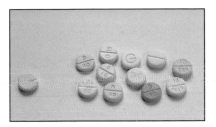

The blue 10mg Valium tablet is shown to the left of a sample of non proprietary products of the same strength

Actual size of 10mg Valium tablet

MEDAZEPAM (LONG-ACTING) – Medazepam is produced in capsules under the proprietary name Nobrium. They are either orange and yellow (5mg), or orange and black (10mg), and both are marked with the capsule strength and the name 'ROCHE'.

Nobrium capsules contain the drug medazepam in two strengths; an orange and yellow capsule of 5mg and an orange and black capsule of 10mg

Actual size of Nobrium capsules

HYPNOTICS

Hypnotics can be divided into three groups: short-acting, intermediate-acting and long-acting. **Short-acting** hypnotics have effects which last for about six hours. Few side-effects are experienced the next day but with continued use anxiety levels during the day may rise and insomnia return. **Intermediate-acting** hypnotics are effective for between six to 10 hours. Insomnia is less likely to occur but there may be some longer-lasting side-effects. **Long-acting** hypnotics have a prolonged effect which may continue into the next day. Accumulation of the drug may occur with repeated use.

Benzodiazepines have become the preferred hypnotic because it was thought that there were fewer adverse effects, interaction with other drugs and potential for abuse than with other types, particularly barbiturates.

However, dependence does occur and because of this benzodiazepine hypnotics should only be prescribed for insomnia when it is severe, disabling or causing extreme distress.

The cause of insomnia should be established in the first instance and any underlying problems treated. Again short-term prescribing is recommended. Tolerance develops within three to 14 days and indiscriminate and long-term administration has resulted in dependence. Any attempt to withdraw could produce conditions worse than the original symptoms.

Rohypnol tablets contain the drug flunitrazepam of 1mg strength

Actual size of Rohypnol tablets

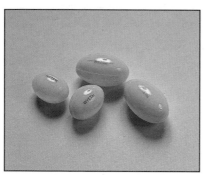

Normison contains the drug temazepam in two strengths; 10mg and 20mg

Actual size of Normison 10mg capsule

Actual size of Normison 20mg capsules

A sample of the medicinal preparations, in capsule form, produced by a number of manufacturers under the generic title temazepam. The capsules may contain the drug in a liquid, or more recently in gel. The size of the capsule denotes its strength which varies from 10mg to 30mg

Actual size of temazepam capsules

The benzodiazepines marketed as hypnotics include:

FLUNITRAZEPAM (INTERMEDIATE-ACTING) – Flunitrazepam appears in the brand name Rohypnol as 1mg purple diamond-shaped scored tablets marked 'ROHYPNOL'.

TEMAZEPAM (INTERMEDIATE-ACTING) – Temazepam is produced as a generic product in the following: 10, 15, 20 and 30mg liquid-filled capsules; 10 and 20mg tablets; an elixir; 10, 15, 20 and 30mg gel-filled capsules; and 2, 5, and 10mg green soft gelatine capsules marked UO, EO and 10 respectively.

Temazepam also appears under the brand name Normison in yellow capsules of 10mg strength marked N10 and 20mg yellow capsules marked N20.

FLURAZEPAM (LONG-ACTING) – Flurazepam appears in the brand name Dalmane as capsules of two strengths; grey and yellow 15mg, or black and grey 30mg. Both are marked with their strength and the word 'ROCHE'.

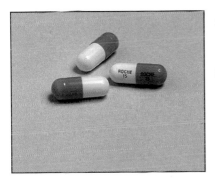

Dalmane capsules contain the drug flurazepam. The grey and pale yellow capsules have a strength of 15mg

Actual size of Dalmane capsules, both 15mg and 30mg

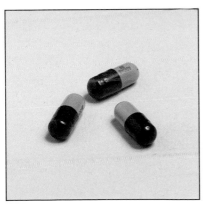

Dalmane capsules coloured black and grey have a stronger concentration of 30mg of flurazepam

NITRAZEPAM (LONG-ACTING) – Nitrazepam is produced in 5mg tablets and a liquid mixture as generic products. It also appears in tablets and capsules under the brand name Mogadon. The tablets are white and scored and marked with two crescent shapes resembling eyes, and the word 'ROCHE'. The capsules are purple and black and marked with 'ROCHE 5'. Both are of 5mg strength.

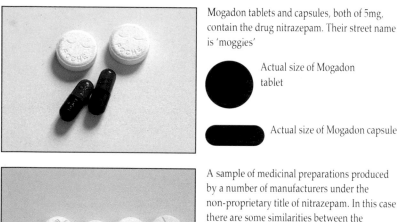

Mogadon tablets and capsules, both of 5mg, contain the drug nitrazepam. Their street name is 'moggies'

Actual size of Mogadon tablet

Actual size of Mogadon capsule

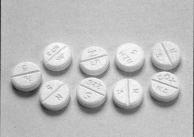

A sample of medicinal preparations produced by a number of manufacturers under the non-proprietary title of nitrazepam. In this case there are some similarities between the products although the markings vary

EFFECTS Benzodiazepines have fewer side-effects than barbiturates and are less likely to interact with other drugs. Side-effects are normally mild and include drowsiness, light-headedness and confusion. Like the effects of alcohol, they can also release inhibitions so that some people become talkative and excitable, hostile and even aggressive.

DEPENDENCE AND WITHDRAWAL Benzodiazepines have only a slight depressive effect on the central nervous system, but tolerance can develop, and with regular use barbiturate-type dependence may result. Such dependence is usually psychological. Physical dependence may also be present, the extent of which would vary from person to person.

Withdrawal can be achieved in many cases fairly easily and

relatively safely, if done gradually. There may be more problems with short-acting benzodiazepines and also where use has been long term. Particular problems occur if the supply of the drug is suddenly stopped.

Some individuals suffer quite severely and withdrawal symptoms can include insomnia, anxiety including panic attacks, loss of appetite and body weight, nausea, tremor, perspiration and perceptual disturbances. A person may be suddenly confronted with the original symptoms which precipitated use of the drug. These could last for weeks or months. Abrupt withdrawal could produce confusion, convulsions and psychosis.

A number of surveys have been undertaken in the UK in an attempt to assess the extent of the dependence problem arising from the legal prescribing of benzodiazepines. Estimates suggest that up to 3.5 million people could be considered potentially at risk from dependence, and as many as a million adults could to some extent be dependent on benzodiazepines.

ABUSE Benzodiazepine tranquillisers and hypnotics are not produced illegally and when misused, generally originate – by prescription or theft – from a licit source.

With so many being prescribed, they are usually more readily available than with most other drugs. How many bathroom or medical cabinets contain unused supplies of benzodiazepines which parents have forgotten about, and perhaps are also unaware of their misuse potential?

The euphoric effect from benzodiazepines varies quite significantly from drug to drug but all are enhanced when taken with alcohol. Abuse has increased, particularly amongst established addicts whose primary drugs of abuse are opiates.

The worrying trend of injecting benzodiazepines which heightens the effects of the drug is also said to be on the increase. The liquid and gel from some capsules are used for injection. This is not only inherently dangerous as the substances are not intended for injection but there are the added risks of HIV infection from sharing equipment.

OVERDOSE Fatal overdosing on benzodiazepines is rare, as this would need a very high consumption. But if taken with alcohol or other drugs, the dangers of an overdose increase considerably.

CONTROLS A prescription is required under the Medicines Act to obtain benzodiazepine tranquillisers or hypnotics from a community pharmacy. In addition, since 1986 a number of benzodiazepines have been brought within the control of the Misuse of Drugs Act as Class C drugs.

A person may be in possession of one of these drugs if properly prescribed for him. However, even without a prescription, possession is only unlawful when it is not in the form of a medicinal product. Tablets which are crushed, either to prepare for injecting or in an attempt to prevent identification, would not constitute a medicinal preparation and possession would be illegal.

Only authorised persons may supply to another, otherwise possession with intent to supply, and supplying benzodiazepines are offences. It is not an offence under the Act to import and export the drugs providing they are contained in the form of a medicinal product.

| Drugs | Class | Medical uses | Dependence potential | | Tolerance | Duration of effect (in hours) | Methods of administration licit and illicit | Possible effects[1] | Possible effects of overdose[1] | Possible withdrawal symptoms | Medical preparation in which individual drugs occur[2] |
			Physical	Psychological							
Barbiturates	B	Sleeping tablets, anaesthetic, anti-convulsant, relief of migraine	High	High	Yes	1 to 16	Oral, injection	Euphoria, slurred speech, disorientation, drunken behaviour (without smell of alcohol)	Shallow respiration, cold and clammy skin, weak and rapid pulse, coma, possible death (not applicable to benzo-diazepines)	Anxiety, insomnia, tremors, delirium, convulsions, possible death (less severe with benzo-diazepines)	Amytal, Sodium Amytal, Soneryl, Tuinal, Seconal, Phenobarbitone
Benzodiazepines	C	Relief of anxiety, sedation, anti-convulsant, muscle relaxant	Fairly high	High	Yes	4 to 8	Oral, injection				Valium, Librium, Nobrium, Mogadon, Ativan, Normison, Dalmane, Rohypnol

[1] The effects of individual drugs may be enhanced when taken with alcohol or in combination with other drugs.

[2] This list is not exhaustive. Some of these products are no longer supplied on the National Health Service. Though in some cases generic equivalents may be prescribed, these may differ in form, colour and manufacturer's markings, making visual identification even more difficult.

STIMULANTS

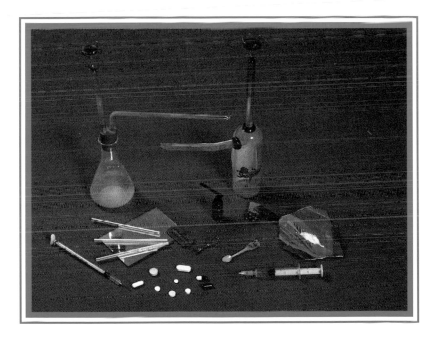

STIMULANTS

GENERAL DESCRIPTION

Stimulants are those drugs which work by stimulating the central nervous system. They are called 'uppers' by drug misusers as they produce almost immediate energy and strength, even when the user feels tired and listless.

There are many mild, socially accepted stimulants which are not often thought of as drugs. Drinks like coffee, tea or Coca-Cola contain caffeine, the most widespread stimulant used in this country.

Synthetic stimulants, notably the amphetamines, are manufactured both pharmaceutically and illicitly. They are considerably stronger and are widely abused.

The best-known and most powerful stimulant of all is cocaine. As street supplies have increased, and misuse in combination with other drugs has grown, cocaine is becoming a major cause of concern.

The stimulants produce euphoria, excitement and increased activity, and can enable the user to feel wide-awake and go without sleep for long periods. But when regularly used, the body builds a natural toler-

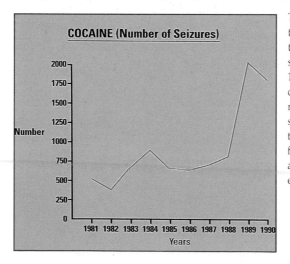

COCAINE (Number of Seizures)

Number

2000
1750
1500
1250
1000
750
500
250
0

1981 1982 1983 1984 1985 1986 1987 1988 1989 1990

Years

The two graphs show why there is growing concern over the deteriorating illicit cocaine situation in the UK. Since 1981 annual quantities of cocaine being recovered have risen dramatically with 1990 seizures running parallel with that of heroin. Provisional figures for 1991 show the amount of cocaine seized exceeded one tonne!

ance, and while physical dependence is generally not thought to result, serious psychological dependence can easily be acquired.

COCAINE

SOURCE Cocaine is derived from the leaf of the coca plant (*Erythroxylum Coca*) which grows abundantly in the mountainous regions of South America, such as in Columbia, Bolivia, Peru and Brazil, and also in Taiwan, Java, India and parts of Africa. For centuries, the leaves have been chewed by South American Indians, either in religious ceremonies or to relieve hunger and exhaustion when working in the Andean mountains. Since they seldom contain more than 2 per cent cocaine, and so only small amounts of the drug are consumed, serious problems have not been associated with such use.

HISTORY About 100 years ago, a technique was discovered to extract cocaine hydrochloride, an effective local anaesthetic, from the coca leaf. Cocaine use quickly spread far and wide and in many forms.

It was popularised as an ingredient of 'Angelo Mariano's Tonic Wine', enjoyed by rich and poor alike. Among its advocates were writers Alexandre Dumas, Jules Verne and Emile Zola; inventor Thomas Edison and even Pope Leo XIII.

Other commercial products followed – cold cures and chewing gum, cigarettes and countless patent medicines. The best known of all was Coca-Cola, from which the coca content was only removed in 1903.

Sigmund Freud recommended cocaine for treating depression, until

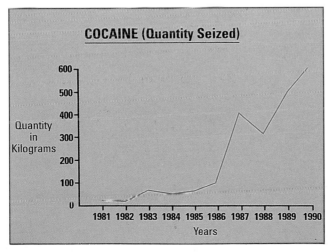

Cocaine is produced from the leaves of the coca plant

he recognised the addictive dangers. It was used widely as a local anaesthetic in eye, ear, nose and throat surgery, before safer synthetic substitutes were discovered.

Cocaine has always had a special appeal for the wealthy and influential. Just as the fictional detective Sherlock Holmes used cocaine (as did his creator, Sir Arthur Conan Doyle), so, more recently, it has been among the upper socio-economic élite that cocaine has been championed as the champagne or caviar drug.

Now, with increased availability, cocaine and its compelling addictive qualities is spreading to all sections of society.

PRODUCTION PROCESS AND RECOGNITION The diagram on page 79 shows the stages of production from coca leaves to cocaine hydrochloride – the salt form of the drug. During the process the drug is switched from the base form to the salt form a number of times which assists purification.

Coca paste, 'pasta' or 'basuco' is an intermediate product in the process. This is smoked in some South American countries and has been exported in that form, particularly to the USA. Smoking coca paste is recognised as a particularly serious form of misuse. It is made even more hazardous by the harmful impurities and chemicals that still remain in this unrefined product. Coca paste has reached the UK as evidenced by one exceptional seizure.

The final stage is cocaine hydrochloride and it is imported almost exclusively in this form into the UK. This is a bitter-tasting white crystalline powder which sparkles in the light, giving rise to such slang names as 'snow', 'sleigh-ride' and 'white lady'.

The purity of cocaine hydrochloride is on average about 85 per cent at importation and ranges from between 30 and 60 per cent at street level. The most frequently encountered adulterants (cutting agents) are mannitol and lactose, and to a lesser extent lignocaine and procaine.

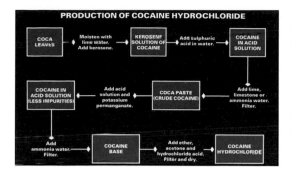

Production diagram showing how coca leaves are processed into cocaine hydrochloride. This is usually done in South America, before the drug is exported, but both coca leaves and coca paste are sometimes smuggled out for processing elsewhere

The latter two substances are local anaesthetics and if tasted will produce localised anaesthesia in a similar way to that of cocaine.

Cocaine hydrochloride is unsuitable for smoking as it is non-volatile and much of the active drug is destroyed at high temperatures. To produce a smokable product the salt has to be brought back to its base form by neutralising the hydrochloride or acid part. The resulting product is known as 'crack' or 'freebase' depending on the production method used.

An increasing number of small street-level seizures of crack are being made in the UK. Contrary to media reports, it is not a new drug, nor a synthetic cocaine, nor even a cocaine derivative. It is a base form of the drug and chemically identical to freebase which appeared on the drug scene at least 10 years ago. It differs from freebase only because of the way it is prepared.

The freebase process has been used for several years and consists of dissolving cocaine hydrochloride in water with an alkali which releases the base. A solvent such as ether is then used to capture the base. As the ether evaporates a residue of freebase cocaine, a white

The coca leaves are picked by the Andean peasants and dried before being processed into cocaine hydrochloride

Cocaine hydrochloride, the most common form of cocaine, is a deceptively innocent-looking sparkling white crystalline powder

Recent importations of cocaine hydrochloride powder into the UK have been in the form of compressed blocks measuring 18 × 12 × 2cm. The blocks, which look more like polystyrene, do not have the distinctive appearance of cocaine hydrochloride

Cocaine freebase is a white powdery substance which could have a very high purity level

powdery substance, is obtained. The purity does vary and can be as high as 95 per cent pure or even higher.

As ether is a highly flammable solvent, the process involves the risk of fire and explosion. It is particularly hazardous if attempts are made to speed up the process of evaporation by gentle heating. This method has mainly been restricted to users who wish to produce smaller quantities of more highly refined freebase for their own use. Freebase has been encountered on many occasions.

A more recent method is favoured by dealers who wished to produce smokable cocaine as quickly as possible for commercial purposes. There are several variations to the production process but all involve heating the cocaine hydrochloride with water and an alkali. This neutralises the hydrochloride part and the product, when dried, is known as crack.

The purity and appearance of crack varies according to the method used. The purity is generally higher than that of cocaine hydrochloride and ranges from between 80 to 100 per cent pure. It may appear in various forms, from a yellow oily-looking, rock-like lump similar to chips of broken porcelain or marble to white granules similar to dried milk which crumble into a powder when pressed between the fingers. Its slang names include 'rock', 'wash' and 'flake'.

Crack may vary quite significantly depending on the production process. Its appearance may be, as in the photograph, from yellow/beige rocky lumps to a white powdery substance similar to freebase

HOW COCAINE IS TAKEN The most common way to take cocaine hydrochloride is 'snorting' or sniffing the drug into the nostrils and absorbing it into the bloodstream via the nasal mucous membranes.

A small quantity is usually placed on a mirror, chopped into a fine powder and put into a 'line' with a razor blade. This 'line' is then sniffed into the nostrils through a straw, glass tube or banknote, often of high denomination. Prolonged 'snorting' causes ulceration and perforation of the nasal septum.

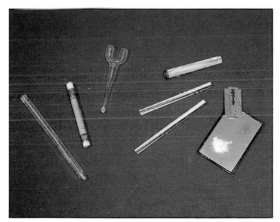

A selection of items used to prepare and 'snort' (sniff) cocaine

Cocaine is also injected, but this rapidly destroys the skin tissues and causes ulcers.

Crack can be smoked in cigarettes or pipes after mixing with tobacco or marijuana. These are not particularly efficient methods of consumption as most of the drug is destroyed by the high temperatures generated in a cigarette or tobacco pipe.

For these reasons users prefer to smoke crack by means of a water pipe. These are available commercially or can be constructed easily by using suitable laboratory glassware.

Homemade pipes are more likely to be found at street level and these are made from soft drink cans, plastic and glass bottles, glass tubing, drinking glasses and aluminium foil. The drug is heated gently in the 'pipe' until it vapourizes when the fumes can be inhaled. The source of heat may be a lighted match, cigarette lighter or butane/propane gas torch. The process of smoking both freebase and crack is generally known as 'freebasing'.

EFFECTS AND DANGERS Sniffing or injecting cocaine can cause a strong psychological dependence, but are not thought to involve physical dependence. (Injection of cocaine has generally been associated with the subcutaneous route – under the skin – as opposed to intravenous injection common with heroin.) It produces a period of

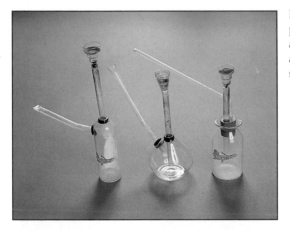

Pipes for smoking cocaine are produced commercially, and although this is illegal, there are still many sources of supply

Users at street level are more likely to make their own pipes from a variety of articles. The presence of these items, which normally would have a quite innocent purpose, could be indicative of misuse

intense well-being, exhilaration and euphoria. This can be followed by feelings of agitation, anxiety or fear and even hallucinations when the user feels threatened.

Large doses cause sleeplessness, hallucinations, tremors and convulsions. Paranoid delusions can lead to violent behaviour. Respiratory troubles, digestive disorders and sensations of insects crawling on or under the skin occur. The pupils become dilated, and heart rate and blood pressure increase.

Smoking cocaine is simply a means of getting the drug into the brain as quickly as possible. The intense and almost immediate euphoric experience accompanied by exaggerated feelings of well-being is short-lived. The effects may wear off within as little as 12 minutes to be replaced by feelings of depression and anxiety.

It is sometimes alleged that new users become instantly dependent on crack. Although some individuals are more susceptible than others, instant dependence is probably the exception. But the nature of the substance which brings about such extreme levels of euphoria and distress is bound to encourage some to seek further satisfaction. Continued use and increasingly larger doses may result in an enormous compulsive craving and complete psychological dependence on the drug.

Experts in countries where crack smoking is a regular feature of drug misuse are convinced that it also results in a form of physical dependence with withdrawal symptoms similar to heroin being common.

Another growing danger is 'mixing the gravy' or combining cocaine and heroin in a 'speedball'. These are the two most compatible drugs

Cocaine hydrochloride is rarely available at street level. Although it is usually sold by the gram, the paper wrap shows about 0.5gm which would cost between £30 and £50. The other packaging contains 'rocks' of crack which are increasingly being sold at street level. Each packet would cost between £25 and £30 for an addict, so when both are available such mixing is inevitable. The result can be a very dangerous dual addiction.

OVERDOSE In cases of overdose from any form of cocaine misuse, heart and breathing malfunctions have proved fatal.

THE COCAINE CULTURE Cocaine has developed its own fashions, with specially made spoons, razors, mirrors and containers sold as jewellery, both in the USA and now in this country. It is an offence to supply or offer to supply such items for administering or preparing cocaine for the purpose of administering it.

Several books have also appeared, promoting cocaine and detailing its use. Such publications are only illegal if they fall within the provisions of the Obscene Publications Act 1959.

CONTROLS Medical use has been largely restricted, though cocaine is still used with diamorphine (heroin) for the relief of severe pain, notably in terminal illness. Occasionally it is prescribed by Home Office-licensed doctors in treating addiction.

Cocaine, including the leaves of the coca plant and the various salts of the drug, is categorised as a Class A drug under the Misuse of Drugs Act.

SLANG NAMES Street slang terms for cocaine include:

Coke	Charlie	Candy	Charlie coke
'C'	Big 'C'	Corrine	Sleigh-ride
Flakes	Snow	Gold dust	Nose candy
Star dust	Happy dust	Bernice	White lady
Carrie	Cecil	Cholly	Crack
Wash	Base	Rock	

AMPHETAMINES – GENERAL

HISTORY Amphetamine is a synthetically produced stimulant that was developed in Germany during the 1880s. At first, like heroin, it was considered safe, with valuable medical qualities and no risk of addiction.

Benzedrine inhalers were introduced in the 1930s to treat asthma, and during the Second World War amphetamine tablets were given to battle-fatigued soldiers. With so many people exposed to the drug, the dangers of regular amphetamine use became evident.

This did not prevent the spread of amphetamine misuse and in the 1960s there was wide publicity about young people, especially in London's West End clubs, taking large quantities of Drinamyl tablets – known as 'purple hearts' because of their shape and colour. These tablets have since been withdrawn, but amphetamine abuse has continued.

MEDICAL USE A number of compounds in the amphetamine group have been used in medicine as treatments for narcolepsy (severe drowsiness), hyperactivity in children, epilepsy, and Parkinson's disease, depression or severe tiredness, and as an appetite suppressant for the obese. They have been prescribed as a fluid for drinking and in ampoules for injection, but more usually they are supplied in tablet or capsule form to be swallowed.

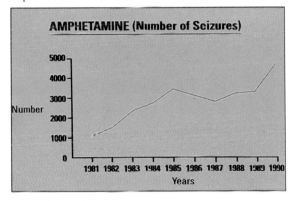

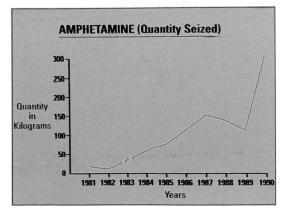

The two graphs show the constant rise of both the number of seizures and the quantity of illicit amphetamine seized in the UK since 1981. Provisional figures for 1991 show a further increase in the amount seized to 325 kilograms. Except for the misuse of cannabis, it is the only drug which has spread equally across the whole of the UK

They varied in the range and intensity of effects they caused although most produced a degree of stimulation. Generally speaking they are not used to a great extent today because of the problems in the past and the potential for misuse. Prescription is discouraged whenever possible.

EFFECT AND DEPENDENCY Typical amphetamine-type effects and dependency resulting from misuse are described in the next section under amphetamine sulphate.

CONTROLS The majority of amphetamine or amphetamine-like substances come under Class B of the Misuse of Drugs Act. In inject-able form they become Class A. Some of the milder drugs have been brought under the control of the Act as Class C drugs, or are still not subject to control apart from the Medicines Act 1968.

SOURCE Many of the amphetamines and amphetamine-like substances which have a potential for abuse and are listed below are pharmaceutically produced. However, current supplies are over-whelmingly manufactured illegally in backroom factories. Only basic equipment and a fairly limited knowledge of chemistry are required to produce amphetamine. The necessary chemicals are readily available in this country.

AMPHETAMINE SULPHATE

The most common homemade amphetamine is amphetamine sulphate, sometimes found in tablet form, in capsules or as a loose powder in a variety of different textures and colours. It predominantly appears as a coarse-textured off-white powder. The purity of the drug at street level is extremely low at around 6 per cent. It contains many impurities from the production process in addition to other substances which are added later. The main bulking agents are sugars such as lactose, glucose and mannitol. Less common additions are caffeine and paracetamol.

It may be consumed orally, by injection or by 'snorting' in the manner of cocaine. Established users are more likely to inject and this form of administration appears to be on the increase, even amongst new users.

New users may dissolve the drug in a soft or alcoholic drink. Other methods of consumption include rubbing it onto the gums or 'dabbing' i.e. sucking from a wet finger which has been dabbed into the drug.

Amphetamine sulphate remains the only illicit drug (with the exception of cannabis) which has permeated all areas of the UK to an equal extent.

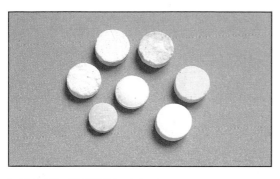

Amphetamine sulphate is sometimes found in tablet form

Amphetamine sulphate powder has appeared in capsules. Mixtures of amphetamine, shredded LSD paper squares and MDMA (ecstasy) have also been detected in capsules

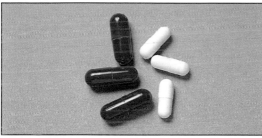

A selection of illicit amphetamine sulphate powders. The drug may appear in a variety of colours and textures. It is easily produced and readily available at street level. It presents a serious and growing threat

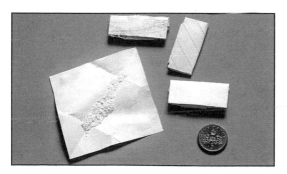

Amphetamine sulphate is usually sold in gram wraps which would cost between £10 and £15. It is often double-wrapped with cling film which enables users to hide it under their tongue to prevent detection

EFFECTS The effects of taking amphetamine sulphate vary widely from person to person, and according to circumstances and environment. An occasional user may take weeks to consume less than a gram, while heavy users who have a tolerance might take up to 2 grams a day.

The 'buzz' or 'rush' produced, whether injected or taken orally, brings an overwhelming sensation of euphoria. This may be reflected in elation, nervous excitability, sleeplessness, agitation, talkativeness, aggressiveness, lack of appetite and seemingly unlimited energy. Other effects may include dry mouth and thirst, sweating, palpitations, increased blood pressure, nausea, sickness, headaches, dizziness and tremors.

The effects usually wear off after three or four hours, when the user becomes suddenly tired, irritable, depressed and unable to concentrate. Feelings of confusion, persecution and violence can follow.

DEPENDENCE Psychological dependence develops with prolonged use. It consists of a strong desire to continue taking the drug and a need to use increasing amounts to obtain the same sensations.

Users dependent on the drug are prone to contracting infections and diseases from contaminated hypodermic needles. Their general state of health is often low, and severe depression, mental illness and even suicide can result.

An overdose of amphetamine sulphate increases body temperature and can cause hallucinations, convulsions and possible death.

DEXAMPHETAMINE SULPHATE

In its basic form dexamphetamine sulphate is a white or off-white crystalline powder with a slightly bitter salty taste.

It is prescribed under the proprietary name of Dexedrine and is used medically in the treatment of narcolepsy and in the management of hyperactive children. Dexedrine is produced as a white scored tablet marked 'SKF'. It has a strength of 5mg.

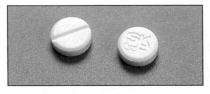

Dexedrine tablets – pharmaceutically produced tablets which contain the drug dexamphetamine, a powerful stimulant

 Actual size of Dexedrine tablet

Dexamphetamine sulphate is a powerful central nervous system stimulant and misuse may result in significant amphetamine-type side-effects, tolerance and dependency (see amphetamine sulphate).

METHYLAMPHETAMINE

Methylamphetamine or methamphetamine is a drug chemically related to amphetamine sulphate but significantly more active. It gained popularity during the 1970s as it became known as a drug which gave a better 'high' than amphetamine. It was associated with bizarre and violent behaviour and interest in the drug declined. In 1989 increasing seizures of methylamphetamine became a matter of serious concern. They reached a peak in that year and since then availability has fluctuated.

The abuse of methylamphetamine is a serious problem in the USA and it is not clear why the trend has not been followed to the same extent in this country.

In appearance methylamphetamine is very similar to amphetamine sulphate and is often sold as good quality amphetamine. Its true identity is normally not established until it has been chemically analysed.

Methylamphetamine is similar to amphetamine in both appearance and chemical composition. It is, however, much more potent. Its availability recently has been unpredictable

The method of administration is similar to amphetamine sulphate but methylamphetamine powder mixed with tobacco in a cigarette can be smoked. This is not an efficient method of consumption because most of the drug is destroyed in the high temperatures of the cigarette before the fumes can be inhaled.

During 1987, as crack smoking was gaining a hold throughout the USA, a new smokable form of methylamphetamine was identified known as 'ice', 'meth', 'crystal', 'glass' and 'icecream'.

Ice is produced from methylamphetamine hydrochloride by a conversion process into clear, glassy, rock-like crystals (hence the

Ice is made from methylamphetamine hydrochloride. These particular crystals were produced in the USA where the process is well established; the largest crystal in the centre is the size of a 5p coin

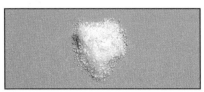

A sample of ice seized in this country

slang names – see the photograph of ice) which are colourless, tasteless and odourless. Depending on the production route of methylamphetamine hydrochloride, the crystals could contain between 90 and 100 per cent pure drug.

Ice is smoked in a specially made small round pipe. It has a stem approximately 150mm in length with a vent hole between the chamber and mouthpiece which allows the hot vapours to be released. A small crystal of ice is placed in the main chamber and heated until it melts. During this time the vent and chamber opening are sealed with the fingers. The vapour is then inhaled.

EFFECTS AND DEPENDENCE The effects and dependence potential of methylamphetamine are similar to that of amphetamine misuse although, as the drug is much stronger, the dangers involved are relatively greater and overdose cannot be discounted. Abuse can result in amphetamine psychosis and schizophrenic symptoms.

Smoking methylamphetamine in the form of ice increases the dangers still further. It results in an instantaneous dose of almost pure drug to the brain which gives a very intense 'rush' followed by a feeling of euphoria for between two and 16 hours, depending on the amount taken. It is also reported that the high is more intense than smoking crack.

A number of adverse side-effects may occur. Body temperature could increase leading to fever and nausea. Rapid cardiac and respiratory rates develop and blood pressure increases. Paranoid delusions and auditory hallucinations may be experienced with both initial and subsequent use. Bizarre, aggressive and psychotic behaviour has been reported in some individuals smoking ice.

When the drug wears off there may be feelings of restlessness, anxiety, irritability and severe depression. Repeated administration can result in compulsive craving for the drug and psychological dependence. (Effects similar to high doses of amphetamine.)

Overdose of methylamphetamine can lead to severe convulsions followed by circulatory and respiratory collapse, coma and death. Smoking in the form of ice can mean that doses are absorbed very quickly giving increased potential for toxic effects. Fatalities have occurred after only small doses suggesting that, like cocaine, there is no safe dose.

EPHEDRINE

Ephedrine is a substance which is chemically similar to amphetamine. It appears as colourless crystals or white crystalline powder It has a bitter taste and is either odourless or has a slight aromatic odour.

MEDICAL USE Ephedrine, alone or with other drugs, appears in a number of prescription-only medicines including those for the treatment of bronchial spasm and airway obstruction in chronic bronchitis or bronchial asthma; nasal decongestants; and allergic conditions e.g. hayfever and nettle rash.

ABUSE Abuse of ephedrine is a fairly recent phenomenon. It appears as a white powder at street level and the method of misuse is similar to that of amphetamine. Users are often not aware of its true identity as it is regularly sold as amphetamine. Only a laboratory analysis would reveal the true nature of the substance.

EFFECTS The effects of misuse and overdose are similar to amphetamine and although prolonged administration is thought to have no cumulative effect, tolerance with dependence has been reported.

CONTROLS Ephedrine is not currently controlled by the Misuse of Drugs Act for the purposes of possession, possession with intent to supply and supply.

It is used in the illicit production of the drug methylamphetamine and it has recently been made an offence to supply ephedrine for this purpose. Companies must provide the Home Office with notification of an intended export to countries outside the European Community. This enables the movement of ephedrine to be monitored in an attempt to prevent illegal manufacture of methylamphetamine.

Possession of large quantities of ephedrine may be an important indicator of illicit production. Smaller quantities seized by the police at street level have almost certainly been diverted from this production process and distributed as an amphetamine product.

METHYLPHENIDATE

Methylphenidate is prescribed for narcolepsy, physical and mental lethargy, fatigue associated with depression and, paradoxically, in the treatment of hyperactive children.

Abuse may cause amphetamine-type dependence, and overdose can result in hallucinations, convulsions and coma.

This drug is produced as a white scored tablet marked 'A/B' on one side and 'CIBA' on the other, of 10mg strength and under the proprietary name Ritalin.

PEMOLINE

Pemoline has effects between those of caffeine and amphetamine, and is prescribed for depression, fatigue and some types of epilepsy.

Side-effects are less serious than with many amphetamines, though large doses cause adverse effects.

Pemoline is contained in the brand name preparation Volital which is a small white scored tablet of 20mg strength. It can only be obtained on prescription.

It is also produced in this country for export in the form of a small yellow tablet marked with the relevant manufacturer's code. Seizures have been made in this country indicating illicit diversion.

Pemoline has also been illicitly manufactured and distributed.

CONTROLS Pemoline is a Class C drug under the Misuse of Drugs Act 1971. It is not an offence to import or export the drug and only an offence to possess it if it is not in the form of a medicinal product i.e. illicitly produced pemoline powder. It is, however, an offence to supply to another (other than authorised persons) and possess the drug with intent to supply.

ANORECTICS OR 'SLIMMING AIDS'

Several drugs are specifically classed as anorectics, or substances which suppress the need to eat. They are prescribed in the treatment of obesity and, like amphetamines, stimulate the central nervous system. They should only be prescribed for short periods as tolerance develops with continued use.

Anorectics are liable to misuse and may result in dependence. Overdose effects are similar to those of amphetamine.

Anorectics include:

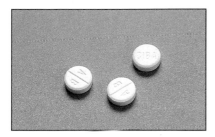

Ritalin tablets containing the drug methylphenidate. They can now be obtained only by special order and so are less frequently encountered

 Actual size of Ritalin tablet

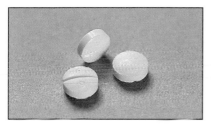

Volital tablets – small tablets which contain 20mg of pemoline

Actual size of Volital tablet

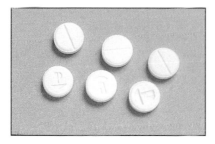

Pemoline tablets produced for export find their way onto the illicit market

DIETHYLPROPION – Apisate is a yellow tablet marked 'WYETH', of 75mg strength. Tenuate Dospan is a white scored elongated tablet marked 'MERRELL', of 75mg strength.

PHENTERMINE – Duromine capsules are coloured grey/green (15mg), or maroon/grey (30mg). Both are marked with the strength and the word 'DUROMINE'. Ionamin capsules are grey/yellow (15mg) or yellow (30mg).

MAZINDOL – Teronac are white 2mg scored tablets marked 'TERONAC'.

DEXFENFLURAMINE – Adifax capsules are white 15mg capsules marked 'S5614' containing dexfenfluramine hydrochloride.

FENFLURAMINE – Ponderax capsules are clear and blue capsules marked 'PxPA60' enclosing white pellets containing 60mg of fenfluramine hydrochloride.

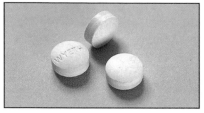

Apisate tablets contain the drug diethylpropion. They may be prescribed as part of a weight-loss programme

 Actual size of Apisate tablet

Tenuate Dospan tablets also contain the drug diethylpropion. Because of their potential for misuse, they have been brought within the control of the Misuse of Drugs Act

 Actual size of Tenuate Dospan tablet

Duromine contains the drug phentermine in two strengths, 15mg and 30mg

 Actual size of Duromine capsules

Ionamin also contains the drug phentermine in two strengths, 15mg and 30mg

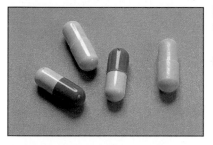 Actual size of Ionamin capsule

Teronac contains the drug mazindol in a white tablet of 2mg strength

 Actual size of Teronac tablets.

Adifax contains 15mg of the drug dexfenfluramine hydrochloride

Actual size of Adifax capsule

Ponderax capsules each containing 60mg of fenfluramine hydrochloride, a drug related to amphetamine

Actual size of Ponderax capsule

Phentermine, diethylpropion and mazindol are amphetamine-like drugs and Class C under the Misuse of Drugs Act. It is an offence to possess, possess with intent to supply and supply these drugs unless authorised to do so.

Neither the drug dexfenfluramine nor fenfluramine are controlled by the Misuse of Drugs Act although both Adifax and Ponderax can only be obtained on prescription.

The Home Office previously licensed slimming clinics to possess and supply certain types of drugs. However, growing concern regarding abuse of this situation resulted in authorisations not being renewed.

The position is still not satisfactory and the Home Office continues to be concerned regarding the manner in which certain slimming clinics operate, as well as the doctors employed by them.

METHYLENEDIOXYMETHYLAMPHETAMINE – 'ECSTASY'

The inclusion of methylenedioxymethylamphetamine (MDMA) or 'ecstasy' at this point in the book i.e. at the end of the stimulants and before hallucinogens, reflects the fact that the drug falls somewhere between the two drug types. It is closely related to both amphetamine and mescaline and is described as a psychedelic drug with stimulant properties.

The abuse of ecstasy has shown a rapid increase in the UK since the mid-1980s alongside the re-emergence of LSD. Both drugs to some extent have been connected to the acid house or pay party scene. Together with amphetamine, the three drugs have been referred to as the 'dance' drugs and are now strongly linked to the developing 'rave' youth culture.

Ecstasy, in particular, is currently a growing cause of concern amongst doctors and other professionals in the field. Provisional seizure figures show that some 252,000 doses of ecstasy were seized in the UK in 1991 compared with approximately 40,000 in both 1989 and 1990. This level of availability and the unpredictability of the effects of the drug have highlighted the serious and even fatal consequences which may result from its misuse.

HISTORY MDMA was first patented in Germany by E. Merck and Co in 1914 as an appetite suppressant but was never marketed. The drug has no current medical use but during the 1970s it was used by American psychiatrists who contended that it was a valuable and safe aid to counselling and therapy. These contentions did not prevent the banning of MDMA in 1985 by US legislation.

Non-medical use of the drug was first reported in western USA in 1968. It appeared as a street drug in the early 1970s and spread rapidly. Abuse is now widespread and well established in the USA but the drug has only started to appear in the UK since the mid-1980s.

SOURCE Most of the seizures to date are believed to have originated in Holland although it has also been manufactured in this country. So far three MDMA laboratories have been detected in the UK. Both the chemicals and the level of expertise required to produce this drug appear to be readily available.

RECOGNITION Ecstasy appears in tablets, capsules and powder form. Tablets are the most frequently available. Illicitly produced they may come in a variety of colours, shapes and sizes. The most frequently encountered tablets have been white, off-white, beige to pale yellow. However, pink, green and blue tablets have also come to notice.

Less frequently seen are clear, yellow, pink and red capsules containing white powder, although black and red capsules nicknamed 'Dennis the Menace' have been particularly prominent. MDMA has also been found in legitimate pharmaceutical capsules where the original contents have been emptied and replaced. MDMA in loose powder form is rare.

LSD (shredded paper squares) and amphetamine, individually and mixed, have been sold at street level as MDMA – as well as being mixed with it.

HOW MDMA IS TAKEN MDMA taken by mouth is the preferred method although experimentation by injection and inhalation has also taken place.

EFFECTS MDMA is effective as a single dose of between 75 to 150mg when taken orally. Effects appear between 30 minutes and one hour after a dose is taken and may last for several hours. Because the effects are not immediate there may be a tendency to take further doses which could build up in the body with dangerous consequences.

Initially the user may experience an amphetamine-like 'rush' of euphoria followed by several hours of peacefulness and heightened sensual awareness. Unpleasant visual hallucinations, the so-called 'bad trip' associated with LSD, are generally absent.

The drug is said to improve trust and communication between friends. It increases an individual's self-esteem and self-confidence. Inhibitions disappear. Contrary to some reports, there is no evidence that it is an aphrodisiac.

The user may experience physical effects including dilated pupils, dry mouth and over-stimulation (e.g. insomnia). Of particular concern are the actions of the drug on the heart including increased blood pressure and heart rate. Other effects include tightening of the jaw and feelings of nausea, dizziness and difficulty with bodily co-ordination.

Whether the experience is good or bad depends, like LSD, on the state of mind and mood of the user before taking the drug, who the user is with and the type of environment. Bad experiences are more likely to occur when using higher doses. These may include anxiety,

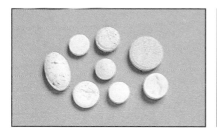

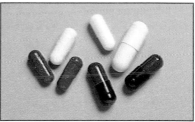

Ecstasy tablets are difficult to identify because of the variation in shape, size and colour. The most well known have the impression of a bird on the face of the tablet and are known as 'Doves'

Ecstasy capsules are not so common. They may additionally contain amphetamine and LSD. The red and black capsules are more familiar and have been named 'Dennis the Menace'

panic, confusion, insomnia, psychosis and visual and auditory hallucinations. 'Flashbacks' of the experience may occur, particularly after using the drug for a prolonged period.

The 'high' obtained with MDMA is often followed by exhaustion and feelings of fatigue, anxiety and depression which may last several days.

Deaths have been attributed to the actions of MDMA. Toxic effects include an abnormally rapid heart rate, pulmonary oedema and respiratory distress, high blood pressure and temperature, internal bleeding and kidney failure. These toxic side-effects, together with psychosis, were thought more likely to occur with doses exceeding 200mg although recent deaths appear to have occurred across a range of dose levels – from one tablet to about five. The long-term consequences of MDMA have not yet been assessed but there have been reports that the drug may cause brain damage.

Tolerance to the effects of MDMA develops with continued use and some dependence is thought to occur but there is no conclusive evidence that the drug has been used compulsively on a long-term basis.

CONTROLS MDMA is a Class A controlled drug under the provisions of the Misuse of Drugs Act 1971. Doctors cannot prescribe it and a licence is required from the Home Office to use the drug for research purposes.

When it started to appear in the UK during the 1980s it was tagged a 'designer' drug. This term was coined in the US to describe a drug which was made by slightly changing the molecular structure of a known controlled drug, thus 'designing' it outside current US legislation.

The description, although still used, is a misnomer in the UK context. The Misuse of Drugs Act was more widely drawn than US legislation and MDMA, together with all other amphetamine-like compounds, were controlled long before the drug became a problem in this country.

METHYLENEDIOXYAMPHETAMINE

Methylenedioxyamphetamine (MDA) is chemically related to MDMA. It was widely misused in the USA during the late 1960s.

MDA is a member of the hallucinogenic amphetamine class and its hallucinogenic effects are stronger than those of MDMA. It is believed that MDA has not been as popular as MDMA because the euphoric effects are less pronounced while the stimulant effects are greater.

MDA appears in similar forms to MDMA i.e. tablets, capsules and powder, and is probably sold as ecstasy. Only a chemical analysis would accurately be able to differentiate between the two.

There had been little evidence of the presence of MDA in the UK until the latter part of 1991 when the drug suddenly appeared in a growing number of seizures.

MDA, like MDMA, is controlled as a Class A drug under the provisions of the Misuse of Drugs Act 1971.

SLANG NAMES The street slang terms for amphetamine-type drugs include:

Amphetamines	= 'A'	Dexedrine	= Dex
	Uppers		Dexy
	Pep pills		Dexies
	Diet pills		
	Jelly beans	Ritalin	= Rities
	Truck drivers		
	Co-pilots	Methylene-	
	Eye-openers	dioxymethylamphetamine	
	Wake-ups		= Big Brown Ones
Methyl-amphetamine	= Meth		Burgers
	Speed		California Sunrise
	Crystal		Disco Biscuits
	Crank		Love Doves
	Ice		New Yorkers
	Glass		M25s
			Pink Skuds
			Dennis the Menace

STIMULANTS

Drugs	Class	Medical uses	Dependence potential Physical	Dependence potential Psychological	Tolerance	Duration of effect (in hours)	Methods of administration licit and illicit	Possible effects[1]	Possible effects of overdose[1]	Possible withdrawal symptoms	Medical preparation in which individual drugs occur[2]
Cocaine	A	Local anaesthetic	Possible	High	Yes	2	Oral, injection, smoked, sniffed	Increased alertness, excitation, euphoria, dilated pupils, increased pulse rate and blood pressure, insomnia, loss of appetite, dry lips	Agitation, increase in body temperature, hallucinations, convulsions, possible death	Apathy, long periods of sleep, irritability, depression, disorientation	
Methylenedioxy-methyl-amphetamine	A		Doubtful	Mild	Yes	Variable	Oral				
Methylenedioxy-amphetamine	A	—	Doubtful	Mild	Yes	Variable	Oral				
Methyl-amphetamine	B		Doubtful	High	Yes	2 to 16	Oral, injection, smoked, sniffed				
Amphetamines	B	Narcolepsy, appetite suppressant	Doubtful	High	Yes	2 to 4	Oral, injection, sniffed				Dexedrine
Methylphenidate	B	Narcolepsy, over-activity in children, anti-depressant	Doubtful	High	Yes	2 to 4	Oral, injection				Ritalin

Drugs	Class	Medical uses	Dependence potential		Tolerance	Duration of effect (in hours)	Methods of administration licit and illicit	Possible effects[1]	Possible effects of overdose[1]	Possible withdrawal symptoms	Medical preparation in which individual drugs occur[2]
			Physical	Psychological							
Pemoline	C	Anti-depressant, over-activity in children	No evidence	Mild	Yes	2 to 4	Oral	Increased alertness, excitation, euphoria, dilated pupils, increased pulse rate and blood pressure insomnia, loss of appetite, dry lips	Agitation, increase in body temperature, hallucinations, convulsions, possible death	Apathy, long periods of sleep, irritability, depression, disorientation	Volital
Diethylpropion	C	Appetite suppressant	Doubtful	High	Yes	2 to 4	Oral				Tenuate Dospan, Apisate
Phentermine	C	Appetite suppressant	Doubtful	High	Yes	2 to 4	Oral				Duromine, Ionamin
Mazindol	C	Appetite suppressant	Doubtful	High	Yes	2 to 4	Oral				Teronac
Dexfenfluramine	POM	Appetite suppressant	Doubtful	Mild	Yes	2 to 4	Oral				Adifax
Fenfluramine	POM	Appetite suppressant	Doubtful	Mild	Yes	2 to 4	Oral				Ponderax

[1] The effects of individual drugs may be enhanced when taken with alcohol or in combination with other drugs.
POM = prescription-only medicine – see page 23.

HALLUCINOGENS

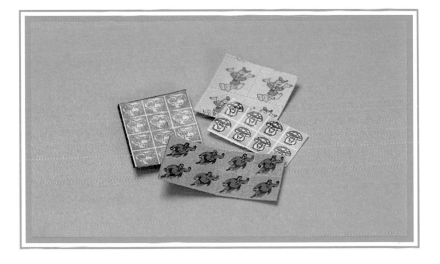

HALLUCINOGENS

GENERAL DESCRIPTION

Hallucinogens are drugs which distort the user's perception of the world. They are also known as 'psychedelics' because they work directly on the functions of the brain. Some derive naturally from plants, while others are produced synthetically in laboratories or backroom factories.

The effects vary widely and can be very unpredictable, depending in particular on the mood and mental attitude of the user, and the environment in which the drugs are taken.

Hallucinogens produce illusions, for example distorting or intensifying the various senses so that sounds are 'seen' or colours 'heard'. They can cause an inability to judge speed, direction or distance, and if taken in large doses are likely to result in hallucinations.

The mental effects of hallucinogens may be completely different each time the drug is taken. They can include illusions, exhilaration, detachment and changes of mood ranging from ecstatic joy to feelings of persecution and panic, when irresponsible and even violent reactions may occur.

The physical effects are generally not serious. Pupils become dilated and the eyes are sensitive to light. The user experiences restlessness and sleeplessness as the effects of the drug wear off.

Although the user may form a psychological dependence, hallucinogens have not been shown to produce any physical dependence.

LSD

The best-known hallucinogen is LSD 25 or lysergic acid diethylamide, commonly known among users as 'acid'. It is a synthetic drug, based on an ergot which has been extracted from fungus that grows on rye grass.

The manufacture of illicit LSD from precursor chemicals is complicated and requires a high level of technical knowledge and expertise. The process produces LSD in crystal form.

HISTORY LSD was first produced in the early 1940s to remove obstructive inhibitions in psychiatric patients. It has since been used to treat chronic alcoholism, character defects and sexual abnormalities, and also in terminal illness. The therapeutic doses were minute, in the region of 25 micrograms. Still, doctors found that the effects could not be properly controlled, and days or weeks after administration, the drug's effects could unexpectedly return.

The unlawful use of LSD developed in the late 1960s and early 1970s when it was associated with the 'psychedelic' era whose followers sought to experience a variety of effects. It was also associated with a number of well-known pop groups.

At the start of this period LSD circulated as an odourless, colourless and tasteless liquid. Amounts for personal use were carried in eye-dropper bottles. These were wrapped in silver paper to keep out the light, which breaks LSD down, and prevent evaporation.

As LSD could be absorbed into any suitable substance, it has since been produced and sold in many different forms. Pieces of blotting paper, sugar cubes and small square flakes of gelatine have all been impregnated with small drops of the drug. It has appeared in microdots, tablets, capsules and powders of various textures and colours.

Microdots, which are tiny tablets about the size of a pinhead, also varied in colour. Because of their size, they were easily concealed. Often they were stuck along a strip of sticky tape, so that they could be snipped off as they were sold.

The average dose of LSD per unit during this period was between 150 and 200 micrograms. Compare this with the dose of 25 micrograms

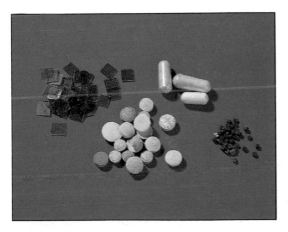

Since the 1960s, LSD has appeared in many forms including tablets, capsules, gelatine squares and microdots. Of those only the latter two are now occasionally seen

given originally to psychiatric patients and the average dose per unit of between 50 and 75 micrograms today. There is no wonder that LSD users experienced serious problems during the 1960s and 1970s.

Use of LSD then declined with very little circulating at street level. In 1985 the police and Customs made minimal seizures of LSD. The following year there was a sudden and dramatic surge in the use and availability of the drug with seizures jumping to over 84,000 dose units – the majority being paper squares. Since then demand has grown across a much wider section of society resulting in some 295,000 dose units being seized in 1990.

Although current trends indicate a growing interest in MDMA, provisional LSD seizure figures for 1991 remain high at 168,000 dose units. The re-emergence of LSD coincided with the acid house or pay party phenomenon which became extremely prominent during 1988–89. Initially these were organised events at unlicensed premises, often empty warehouses or other commercial buildings. The organisers went to great lengths to keep the location of the party from the authorities. Large numbers of young people attended on payment of admission, usually at premises which were not safe or suitable for such purposes.

Pay parties are still frequent events across the country and have now become known as local 'raves'. Many are still unlicensed and some cause problems for the police and local communities. Generally though, recent legislation has encouraged more co-operation between the organisers and the relevant authorities.

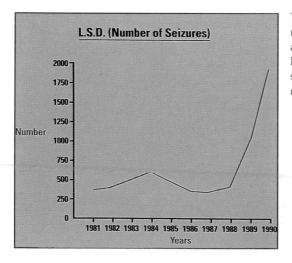

L.S.D. (Number of Seizures)

Number

2000 1750 1500 1250 1000 750 500 250 0

1981 1982 1983 1984 1985 1986 1987 1988 1989 1990

Years

The two graphs highlight the re-emergence of interest in and growing demand for LSD. Provisional figures for 1991 show that some 170,000 dose units of LSD were seized

The current use of LSD is undoubtedly linked to the pay party scene and the drug is imported into the country for distribution at these events. In addition, the use of LSD has also moved into other areas of entertainment such as public houses and clubs.

THE SITUATION TODAY While research continues into the possible uses of LSD for psychotherapy, its potential benefits are balanced by difficulty in controlling its effects, which can be damaging.

Possession of LSD for research purposes must be licensed by the Home Office. Otherwise it is strictly controlled as a Class A drug, and the production, supply and possession of LSD are illegal.

There is no evidence that LSD crystal is being illegally manufactured in this country. Its main source is the west coast of America. The crystal is exported from the USA to Holland which is believed to be the major country for the production of LSD paper doses used in the UK.

There is evidence that paper doses have been produced in this country.

IDENTIFICATION LSD still appears as microdots and gelatine squares, but these are rare.

By far the most popular form of LSD is absorbent sheets of paper which are divided into squares. Each square is approximately 6×6mm and represents one dose. The LSD crystal is dissolved in a liquid and the sheets are impregnated with it. LSD in this form is taken orally.

The sheets are printed with a small motif in each individual square,

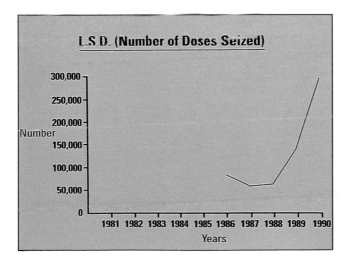

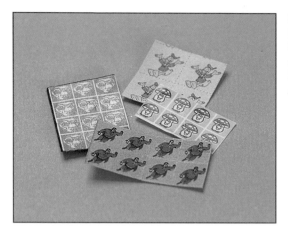

LSD paper squares are currently the most common forms in which the drug appears. The cartoon designs look so innocent and would appeal directly to children

Further examples of cartoon-type designs on recently seized LSD squares

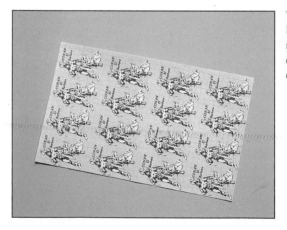

This design depicts 'Conan the Barbarian'. The whole sheet measures 24 × 15cm and contains some 1,000 individual doses of LSD

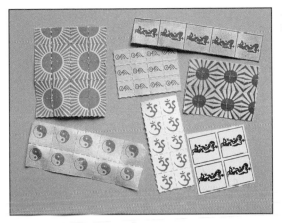

A selection of patterns and symbols

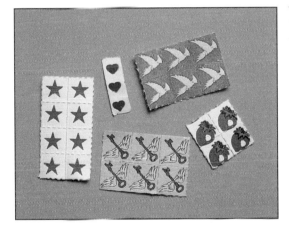

The designs in this group of LSD squares consist of various definite shapes

Designs occasionally appear which are associated with current national or international events. This particular LSD square shows Saddam Hussein. It appeared at the time of the Gulf War

or alternatively, larger motifs which cover a number of squares or the complete sheet. The photograph of the sheet showing 'Conan the Barbarian' measures approximately 15×24cm and contains 1,000 squares or doses of LSD. Each square sells for between £3 and £5 and so the whole sheet would have a potential street value of £5,000.

The motif changes frequently and since the late 1970s there have been over 250 different designs encountered in the UK. It is thought that changing the design acts as a form of 'sell by' date. LSD does deteriorate with time and a newly introduced design shows that it is a fresh supply.

The designs may consist of patterns, symbols, cartoon characters or pictures depicting current events. Many of the designs are attractive and well produced indicating a commercially based enterprise with some printing sophistication.

This type of LSD presentation is disturbing as it is not readily identifiable as a controlled drug. A varied selection of different designs are illustrated and parents in particular should make themselves aware of this form of the drug.

EFFECTS The average current dose per unit of 50 to 75 micrograms of LSD is substantially less than the products experienced during earlier years. This is because the market for LSD has changed. During the 1960s and 1970s LSD's appeal was to those who wished to experience psychedelic illusions and imagery where the drug directed and controlled the psyche and intellectual functions. Now, influenced undoubtedly by the advent of pay parties, a wider market has developed for hallucinogenic LSD which does not involve the dangers and bad experiences of the past. Users wish merely to enhance ongoing experiences rather than to be taken over completely. They expect, using their own terminology, a 'mellow' experience.

However, the method of production is not precise. Whether an individual 'dose' is dropped on each square or the whole sheet is dipped and hung to dry, there are going to be significant variations in strength. The analysis of some doses have been as high as 800 micrograms!

In addition, users may be tempted to consume a number of lower strength doses at intervals over a period of time. The accumulation of the drug taken in this way could also have adverse effects.

Depending on the dose, the effects of LSD begin within an hour of taking the drug, build up over between two and eight hours, and then slowly fade after about 12 hours. It may take several more hours to recover fully after the 'trip' (as it is known) is over.

The LSD experience can be profoundly enjoyable or the complete opposite. The biggest problem is the total unpredictability of the effects of LSD, and of hallucinogens generally. Unlike with many drugs of abuse, even experienced LSD users can have little idea what they are embarking on when they start a 'trip'

DANGERS When LSD produces unpleasant experiences it is called a 'bad trip'. This may include a complete loss of emotional control, disorientation, depression, dizziness and panic. Users can believe they are being attacked and, seeking self-protection, resort to uncontrollable violence. On the other hand they can feel quite invincible and even attempt such acts as flying from the top of buildings, walking on water or stopping oncoming motor vehicles.

There is no reliable evidence of physical harm from excessive use of LSD, but there are psychological dangers. After a 'trip' the user may suffer depression or anxiety. Disturbing 'flashbacks' of LSD experiences may recur weeks or months after the initial use. Short- and long-term psychoses have followed LSD use, but this is rare and usually an inherent mental problem coming to the surface rather than a direct result of the drug.

Great care must be taken when handling LSD, and this can affect a parent or other adult who discovers a supply. The drug can be inadvertently absorbed into the body through a scratch or even by licking a finger which has touched the drug. A minute quantity can have an effect. Protective gloves and a face mask are therefore recommended when handling any substance thought to be LSD.

TOLERANCE Tolerance to LSD develops rapidly, so that it takes much larger doses to achieve the same effects. Because of this, LSD is not usually used on a continuing and regular basis. Tolerance disappears after five to six days.

SLANG NAMES Terms for LSD in frequent use include:

Acid (hence 'acid head' for a regular user)
Blotters
Mellow
Tabs

LSD paper doses are also referred to by their design name e.g. Batman, Smiley

HALLUCINOGENIC ('MAGIC') MUSHROOMS

Two alkaloids, psilocin and psilocybin, are contained in the mushroom *Psilocybe Mexicana*, which grows in Mexico. Both have hallucinogenic properties similar to LSD and mescaline (see page 113).

There are about a dozen varieties of similar hallucinogenic or 'magic' mushrooms that grow in the United Kingdom, the most common being *Psilocybe Semilanceata* (Liberty Cap). The harvesting season is between September and November.

HOW 'MAGIC MUSHROOMS' ARE TAKEN After they are picked, 'magic mushrooms' are either eaten raw, cooked, made into a drink, or dried for later consumption. It takes up to 30 mushrooms to produce an hallucinogenic experience comparable to that from a mild LSD dose.

'Magic mushrooms' that have been picked and dried. The mushrooms contain the drugs psilocin and psilocybin. Up to 30 may be required for an hallucinogenic experience

These tablets, which have the smell and appearance of proprietary yeast tablets, were illicitly made from virtually 100 per cent dried mushroom material. Each tablet is approximately 10mm in diameter by 5mm wide and weighs 4 to 5 grams

EFFECTS The effects range from excitement and euphoria with small doses, to distortions of shape and colour and hallucinations following larger consumption. Often the user feels detached as though looking down from above. There may also be nausea, dizziness, vomiting, diarrhoea and stomach pains.

DANGERS 'Bad trips' can occur, though usually do not last very long. 'Flashbacks' of the original experience are the biggest danger. No other serious problems, such as dependence or withdrawal, are known. Tolerance develops rapidly, which in itself discourages continuous use.

Nevertheless little research has been undertaken into the long-term effects of 'magic mushrooms', and they remain something of an unknown quantity. A real danger is that poisonous mushrooms may be mistakenly gathered and consumed.

CONTROLS Possession of the mushrooms is not in itself against the law, unless they have been processed to prepare them for illicit use. Boiling, slicing or crushing would probably qualify as an offence.

Illicit tablets made from dried mushroom material would clearly be a 'preparation or product' containing a controlled drug and therefore prohibited under the Misuse of Drugs Act.

While psilocybin and psilocin have occasionally been used in psychiatry, they are strictly controlled as Class A drugs.

MESCALINE

Mescaline comes from the peyote cactus, native to Mexico. This is dried and cut into slices known as 'mescal buttons'.

Mescaline was used by Mexican Indians in their religious ceremonies and became known in Europe after the Spanish conquest. Historically, it was either chewed or boiled into a liquid and drunk.

Nowadays mescaline is usually refined into a powder coloured from white to brown. Doses of up to 500mg are taken, with results similar to those produced by LSD.

Like LSD, mescaline is unlikely to produce physical dependence but can cause psychological problems. It is usually swallowed, though it has been reported in injectable form.

Mescaline abuse is not common in this country.

MORNING GLORY

Ololiuqui is an hallucinogenic drug obtained from the black and brown seeds of the Morning Glory plant, which grows in Central and South America. It contains five closely related components all of which have properties similar to LSD.

The seeds are ground into a powder, soaked in water, strained and the liquid is then drunk. It takes 300–400 seeds to produce about 200 micrograms, enough for an average 'trip'. Smaller doses have a sedative effect, while larger ones will cause sickness and diarrhoea.

Like other hallucinogens, the effects are totally unpredictable and may lead to long-term mental illness or serious physical complaints.

Morning Glory seeds are available here, but they are treated with a chemical coating to destroy pests and fungus which causes nausea if consumed.

NUTMEG

Nutmeg is a spice widely used in cooking. The dried kernels, when ground and then swallowed or smoked, stimulate the central nervous system, causing delirium and effects like a mild dose of LSD. Side-effects include dizziness, nausea and general sickness.

STP

STP appeared on the psychedelic scene of the late 1960s, in blue and white capsules. It is a chemical related to amphetamine and mescaline and its effects can last up to 24 hours. STP is more likely to result in a bad experience than the other hallucinogens.

Its chemical name is dimethoxymethamphetamine, shortened to DOM. Little is known about the pharmacological or psychological effects. STP or DOM is a Class A drug.

DMT

DMT is a short-acting hallucinogen, with effects like those of LSD. It is contained in the seeds of plants native to the West Indies and South America.

Powdered, these have been used for centuries by Haitian natives in religious ceremonies as a snuff called *cohoba*. Recently, DMT has been produced synthetically in backroom laboratories as the chemical dimethyltryptamine.

When swallowed, DMT has no effect. It is most commonly taken by smoking the ground seeds mixed with tobacco, parsley leaves or marijuana. It can be injected, but the effect then begins so rapidly that it is too intense for most users.

The effects of a dose, between 60 and 150mg, last up to one hour and the main result is hallucination. DMT does not cause physical dependence but may give rise to psychological problems.

PCP (PHENCYCLIDINE)

Phencyclidine is manufactured as a veterinary anaesthetic. Taken by humans, it has an hallucinatory effect. It is produced illegally and known by drug users as 'PCP', 'angel dust' and 'peace pill'.

The PCP user experiences a trance-like state, with sensations of weightlessness, detachment, diminished body size and an overall distortion of perception. There may also be feelings of overwhelming excitement and strength.

Overdosing can result in vomiting, agitation, disorientation, respiratory depression and convulsions.

In the USA, PCP has been sold as both mescaline and LSD. It can result in a very frightening experience, and when the drug's identity is uncertain, treatment is difficult. While frequently abused in the US, there is little evidence of PCP use here.

KETAMINE HYDROCHLORIDE

Ketamine hydrochloride in its basic form is a white crystalline powder with a characteristic odour.

MEDICAL USE The drug is a short acting general anaesthetic which is used for diagnostic and short surgical operations, or for inducing anaesthesia to be maintained or supplemented by other means e.g. inhalational anaesthetics or other drugs administered intravenously.

Ketamine is administered by intravenous or intramuscular injection and has effective analgesic properties when used in low doses. The only pharmaceutical preparation available in this country for medical use are vials of ketamine hydrochloride in various strengths for injection.

DANGERS Recovery from ketamine administration is relatively slow and may be accompanied by nausea and vomiting. Headache, dizziness and confusion may occur as the patient regains consciousness. Blood pressure and heart rate may be temporarily increased. In addition the period of recovery may include nightmares, hallucinations, irrational and other psychotic behaviour.

Outside the controlled environment of an operating theatre an individual could be in some danger. In the stimulating atmosphere of a disco these adverse effects could be even more enhanced.

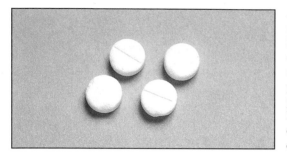

An illicitly produced white scored tablet containing ketamine hydrochloride. It could be confused with many relatively harmless preparations which can be purchased in a pharmacist. Misused, particularly in combination with other drugs, could be extremly dangerous

ABUSE Individuals are misusing this medical preparation, the purpose undoubtedly being to achieve the hallucinatory experience associated with this drug. Ketamine is chemically related to phencyclidine or PCP and the effects may be similar. The dangers are all too apparent, particularly if mixed with alcohol, barbiturates, benzodiazepines or other drugs. Large doses would induce unconsciousness which could lead to cardiovascular failure.

Ketamine has appeared on the street as a white scored tablet. It is thought to be illicitly produced from powder diverted from lawful supplies. Misuse was initially restricted to particular areas but appears to be spreading further afield. The drug could easily be mistaken for a number of other preparations and may even be sold on the pretext that it is another drug. It is a frightening example of users just not knowing what they are buying and taking into their bodies.

CONTROLS Ketamine is not controlled by the Misuse of Drugs Act 1971 but can only be obtained on prescription. Prosecutions could be taken under the Medicines Act for supplying this drug without a prescription. Its medical use is restricted and, in general, supplies should be available only in medical establishments.

SLANG NAMES
K
Special K

HALLUCINOGENS

Drugs	Class	Medical uses	Dependence potential		Tolerance	Duration of effect (in hours)	Methods of administration licit and illicit	Possible effects[1]	Possible effects of overdose[1]	Possible withdrawal symptoms	Medical preparation in which individual drugs occur
			Physical	Psychological							
LSD	A	–	None	Degree unknown	Yes	Variable	Oral	Illusions and hallucinations poor perception of time and distance	Longer, more intense 'trip' episodes, psychosis	Withdrawal syndrome not reported but subsequent psychological disturbance may require treatment	–
Psilocybin Psilocin	A	–	None	Degree unknown	Yes	Variable	Oral				–
Ketamine hydrochloride	–	Short-acting anaesthetic	None	Doubtful	Not known	Variable	Oral, injection	Nausea, vomiting, headaches, dizziness, confusion, increased heart rate and blood pressure	Coma, death		Ketalar

[1] The effects of individual drugs may be enhanced when taken with alcohol or in combination with other drugs.

CANNABIS

CANNABIS

GENERAL DESCRIPTION

Cannabis is used by millions of people throughout the world and is by far the most widely abused illegal drug in the United Kingdom, accounting for over four fifths of all seizures and proceedings. In 1991, some 31 tonnes of cannabis were seized by police and Customs in the United Kingdom.

Pharmacologically, it is a mild hallucinogen. It produces a light-headed euphoria, but except in very large doses does not have the 'trip' effect of psychedelics.

Cannabis comes from a large plant, *Cannabis Sativa*, which grows in hot dry countries, mainly outside Europe. The whole plant, including the roots, is covered with small hairs, although the largest concentration of them is on the flowering parts and top leaves. The hairs produce quantities of a sticky brown resin. The plants are dried and crumbled to produce **marijuana**, or the resin is collected and pressed into cakes known as **hashish**.

Cannabis is usually smoked in large hand-rolled cigarettes which users call 'joints'. It is often mixed with tobacco, especially when hashish, the stronger form, is being used.

Cannabis is without doubt the most controversial of all the illicit drugs. In parts of society it has a degree of acceptance – for example in ethnic groups where use is common in the country of origin, among students, and even for some professional and business people. It is alleged that no fewer than 10 million people in the UK have experimented with cannabis.

Nevertheless, it is fully controlled as a Class B drug and it is an offence to cultivate, produce, supply or possess cannabis, or to allow such use on your premises.

HISTORY Cannabis has been known both for its narcotic qualities and its fibre for thousands of years. It is recorded in a Chinese herbal of 2,737 BC, and was described vividly by the Greek historian Herodotus.

It has been, and remains, widely used in many countries in Africa,

Asia, the Middle and Far East, and North and South America. The stem of the plant is also used in the manufacture of hemp rope and string.

Western countries frequently encountered cannabis, then known as 'Indian hemp', in the days of explorers and colonies. In Culpeper's *English Physician Enlarged* (1792) it was described as 'so well known to every good housewife, that I do not need to write any description of it'. In India, where native use was commonplace while alcohol was shunned, there was a major government commission on the subject in 1893.

Use in this country was mostly restricted to artistic and fashionable circles until the early 1960s when cannabis became much more popular and available, particularly among young people. It was closely associated with pop music and culture, and there was wide debate on whether it should be legalised. Use, supplied by large- and small-scale smuggling, has continued steadily since, showing a regular rise through recent years.

Yet, despite this long history, much remains unknown about the chemical action of cannabis, or the long-term effects of its consumption.

SOURCE Cannabis was originally known in this country as 'Indian hemp', but more recently has been called by its botanical name *Cannabis Sativa*. On the street it has various slang names, which often indicate the place of origin – Lebanese or Moroccan Gold, Paki/Afghan/Nepalese/Kathmandu Black, Mexican Green and so on.

As these names suggest, cannabis is cultivated and harvested in many countries. It is a plant related to nettles and hops which in favourable conditions will grow up to five metres in height.

It grows best in hot sunny regions. Major areas of production include the West Indies, India, Pakistan, Afghanistan, the Middle and Far East, most of Africa, the middle parts of North and South America and other warm areas.

It can be cultivated in the United Kingdom, but the quality is poor even when greenhouses have been used.

There are male and female plants. The males are taller and produce pollen which fertilises the seed-bearing flowers of the female. Both contain the psychoactive ingredient tetrahydrocannabinol, or THC. It is found in all parts except the seed, with the strongest concentration in the flowering shoots of the female plant.

Cannabis seed is sold in angling shops as bait for coarse fishing and also in packets of bird seed.

(Above) The distinctive shape of the cannabis leaf

VARIETIES OF CANNABIS Illegal cannabis is produced in three forms. Marijuana, or herbal cannabis, is a dried tobacco-like substance mainly of West Indian, African, South American or Far Eastern origin. Cannabis resin, commonly called hashish or hash, comes as a resinous slab usually from Asian or Arab sources. There is also a liquid concentrate known as cannabis oil or hash oil.

The amount of THC, and so potency, varies widely according to type and where and how the cannabis plant was cultivated. THC content is likely to range from 5 per cent to 10 per cent in marijuana, up to 20 per cent in cannabis resin and as high as 85 per cent in hash oil.

MARIJUANA

Herbal cannabis or marijuana comes either compressed into blocks or bales or in loose form. Quality and appearance depend on the country of origin.

COMPRESSED CANNABIS – This often includes the whole plant, with the flowering tops, leaves, stalk and seed all cut, crushed and pressed into blocks.

When just the flowering tops of the female plant are used, the cannabis is considered of top quality and is greatly sought after by users.

Jamaican compressed cannabis blocks usually measure about 30×12×5cm. Blocks of **West African** (Nigerian and Ghanaian) **compressed** may be around the same size, or as large as 45×45×10cm and weighing several kilograms. More recently, similar compressed blocks have been imported from Thailand.

Cannabis is often compressed into a shape particular to its country of origin. The **Malawi stick** is a typical example.

When being shipped or smuggled, marijuana is usually found in bales measuring some 60×60×90cm, and coloured brown or pale and even bright green, depending on how long the plant has been cut. The bales are broken down into smaller quantities just before or just after being imported into the country of destination, and as the drug passes down the distribution chain.

Loose herbal cannabis is either the result of compressed cannabis being broken down into smaller quantities or, alternatively, the actual form in which it is produced, such as **St Lucian herbal cannabis**.

Thai sticks are a very distinctive form of herbal cannabis from Thailand. They are sticks about 12cm long, with cannabis shoots twisted around them in a spiral fashion and tied on with a fine cotton-like twine.

Home-grown cannabis plants are usually cut up finely and the result looks rather like cut grass.

Herbal cannabis appears at street level in much smaller quantities than illustrated in the photographs overleaf. In addition, the majority of users are quite unaware and probably not interested in where it originated from. The quality does vary quite significantly and some users are very discriminating.

A particular form of herbal cannabis is sought after for its quality and high THC content. This is known as **Sinsemilla** and consists entirely of female plants. Prior to pollination, the male plants are pulled out so that the female plants do not produce seeds. Instead the flowering heads become enlarged and the THC content increases.

The amount sold as a street deal varies quite considerably but typical quantities are shown together with the various current forms of packaging

Jamaican compressed herbal cannabis usually consists of the whole plant, cut, crushed and pressed into blocks

Nigerian and Ghanaian compressed herbal cannabis is similarly pressed into blocks, although these may vary considerably in size

The Malawi stick is a form of compressed cannabis moulded into a shape peculiar to its country of origin. The usual length is about 15cm

Cannabis from Nigeria, shown here in loose form. It is currently quite common in this country. The stems of the plant can be clearly seen, mixed with the dried leaves

St Lucian cannabis, another example of loose herbal cannabis. Note how green it is compared with the Nigerian variety. This is a sign that it has only recently been harvested

Thai sticks, a most unusual form of herbal cannabis, and one peculiar to Thailand. Such sticks rarely reach the UK

Poor-quality home-grown cannabis, finely cut. The THC content would undoubtedly be fairly low

The greatest concentration of THC is in the flowering tops and top leaves of the female cannabis plant. High quality cannabis in this form is known as Sinsemilla

A growing flowering head of a female cannabis plant

This sample is from a seizure of particularly high quality Sinsemilla. Most of the top leaves have been 'manicured' leaving just the female flowering tops. The source is believed to be mainland Europe!

Herbal cannabis is produced in this way in a number of source countries. Jamaica has been renowned for producing this high-quality form. More recently it has been imported into the UK from mainland Europe where it is thought to be cultivated in quite large quantities under glass.

RESIN

Cannabis resin or 'hashish' also comes in a variety of forms, colours and consistencies depending on the country of origin. It forms in bright sunlight as a sticky, oily coating on the flowering tops of the plants. It is gathered and pressed into blocks, cakes and sticks, which in their final form may be soft and pliant, or hard, dry and powdery.

PAKISTANI AND AFGHAN RESIN – This appears in dark brown or black slabs which measure approximately 22×12×½cm and are often polythene-wrapped to maintain freshness and conceal the smell. Some bear a trademark – either a symbol such as a palm tree, crossed swords or star, hammer and sickle; or else they may have their names stamped on them in Urdu or English, for example 'Bazaar Kabul'.

NEPALESE RESIN – While not common in the United Kingdom, this is regarded as the best-quality cannabis in the world. It takes three main forms. There are black oblong lumps, rougher in texture than Paki Black; sticks, smaller and thinner than a cigarette, known as 'sticks'; and round balls called 'temple balls'.

INDIAN RESIN STICKS – These are dark brown or black, and are produced in a cluster of sticks stuck together. The quality is inferior to Nepalese resin.

LEBANESE GOLD RESIN – This is usually a compressed golden powder wrapped in cotton bags, about 20×8×2½cm. The bag may carry a trademark.

MOROCCAN RESIN – This is now produced in two forms. The traditional golden to greenish-brown slabs of resin are still available; this sometimes takes the form of a loose, fine powder.

More recently it has also been produced in blocks of black resin in three distinct sizes: resin 'tiles' measuring 14½×9½×½cm; resin 'slabs' with approximate measurements of 16×6×2½cm; and resin

Pakistani and Afghan resin – slabs of dark brown or black resin which are hard and brittle. Note the design stamped into the surface of the slab

Indian resin sticks are thin cannabis sticks, dark brown to black in colour, and usually stuck together in a cluster

Lebanese Gold resin comes as a golden powder, compressed into slabs and wrapped in cotton bags

New form of Moroccan resin — 'slabs'

Traditional Moroccan resin is found in compressed slabs, golden to greenish-brown in colour, or else as a loose, fine powder

New form of Moroccan resin   'soap'

New form of Moroccan resin — 'tiles'

Turkish resin in a powder form, light brown in colour

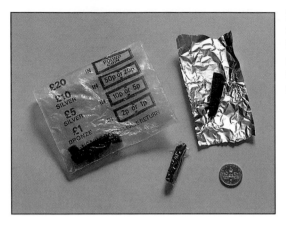

The current trend is to cut street deals of cannabis resin into 'fingers'. A typical quantity is shown together with the various ways in which it is packaged

'soap' measuring approximately 9×7×4cm, the latter two types weighing about 250 grams. The traditional and new forms are chemically identical although, for some reason which is not known at this stage, presentation has undergone a significant change.

TURKISH RESIN – Usually a light brown, loose powder.

Cannabis resin in the quantities shown is rarely evident at street level, although some dealers have been known to cut off user quantities from a slab with a knife as customers ask for it. Now supplies come mainly pre-packaged. This speeds up the transaction and minimises the risk of detection.

Cannabis is usually sold by the 'eighth' or 'sixteenth' of an ounce at street level although a user will never be sure exactly how much he is getting.

CANNABIS OIL

Cannabis oil is extracted from the resin of the cannabis plant and contains a very high concentration of THC. It has been illicitly produced since about 1970. Present supplies are imported from Morocco and Jamaica.

The oil is obtained by suspending flowering heads or resin in a solvent such as acetone, alcohol (often surgical spirit) or petrol. The mixture is filtered and the solvent partially evaporated to leave a brownish substance like treacle or car oil. The thickness or viscosity depends on how much solvent has been evaporated.

A small quantity of hash oil can be spread along the outside of a cigarette, or soaked into a cigarette paper and rolled up with tobacco into a 'joint'. Tobacco can also be impregnated by soaking in hash oil.

CANNABIS – GENERAL

MEDICAL USE Like other wild plants (including the opium poppy and coca plants) cannabis was in the past taken as a herbal remedy. It was used as a treatment for headaches and restlessness, to encourage sleep, for stomach upsets, and as both a stimulant and analgesic agent. It still is in some parts of the world, but has been replaced by modern pharmaceutical medicines in the West.

Until 1973, cannabis was available in community pharmacies as a green liquid tincture. Since then, it has only been allowed to be produced or possessed under licence from the Home Office. Today, lawful cannabis is found solely in scientific establishments for experimental purposes.

HOW CANNABIS IS TAKEN The most common way of consuming cannabis is by smoking. The effect is very quick and the user can regulate the dose consumed. There are two main techniques.

A 'joint' or 'reefer' is a handmade cannabis cigarette using herbal cannabis in place of or with tobacco, or mixing cannabis resin or oil with tobacco. 'Joints' tend to be oversized, and users either purchase large size cigarette papers or stick three or four ordinary papers together. Cannabis smoke is very hot and can burn the throat. To prevent this, large filters, generally made of cardboard, are inserted.

Pipes are found in all kinds of shapes and sizes, mostly improvised and homemade. To reduce the harshness of the smoke, the pipes often have a very long stem or pass the smoke through water in a 'hubble-bubble' pipe, familiar from TV and the cinema. Others use a form of pipe called a 'chillum', which may be no more than a stone with a hole through it.

Cannabis can also be swallowed. As a tea-like drink, made by boiling the drug in water, it is an old African and West Indian health remedy. It can be eaten too, though it has a bitter taste. The most common method is to use it as an ingredient in homemade cakes and sweets.

Unlike with opium, it is not an offence to possess cannabis utensils.

Cannabis oil is concentrated resin in liquid form with a high THC content. It is dark brown in colour and looks like treacle or motor oil

Cannabis may be smoked in a specially made cigarette known as a 'joint' or 'reefer'

A selection of pipes used to smoke cannabis. They are designed to cool the very hot smoke before it is drawn into the lungs

It would, however, be illegal to supply them to someone else so that they could consume cannabis. In addition, the utensils may contain sufficient traces of the drug to qualify as possession, or as evidence to support other charges.

EFFECTS The effects of cannabis depend on the quantity and type consumed, and on the individual's mood, expectations and situation. At first, there are likely to be pleasurable feelings of elation, gaiety and well-being. Cannabis removes inhibitions, and the user may become very excitable, talkative and relaxed.

Large doses can result in lethargy and confusion, with interference to many aspects of mental functioning. Perception, and skilled performance in complex tasks like driving, may be seriously affected.

Acute intoxication can result in severe reactions of apprehension, paranoia and panic. If disturbed, subjects may become aggressive and even violent. Casual and first-time users, or those depressed before consuming excessive doses, are especially susceptible to these disagreeable feelings.

The effects of smoking cannabis start shortly after use, and a strong dose could last several hours. Once the drug wears off, there may be a 'hangover' of headache, nausea and general disability.

Regular, heavy consumption can cause sleep loss or disturbance, irritability and restlessness, decreased appetite, sweating, weight loss, and depression. There is little risk of a fatal overdose of cannabis.

DANGERS There has been much research into whether cannabis is harmful, but with few conclusive results. Generally, it is thought that with occasional use it is no more dangerous than socially accepted drugs like alcohol and tobacco.

Cannabis has an extremely complicated chemical make-up, however, and even after detailed analyses, the effects of all its constituent elements are still not fully understood.

Steps have been taken in some countries towards the decriminalisation of cannabis. In the UK, while there has been an increase in the cautioning of first-time offenders caught with small quantities of cannabis in lieu of prosecution, the idea of legalisation has been resisted.

Much more needs to be known about the substance and its long-term effects before yet another potentially harmful drug comes into general use. Research already indicates adverse psychological effects with both casual and long-term use, and that prolonged consumption may cause organic, and therefore permanent, brain damage. Psychological dependence is a possibility.

Cannabis smoke has a quicker and more damaging effect on the human lung than tobacco, and the risk of lung cancer is greatly increased. There is also evidence that THC reduces the body's capacity to resist infectious diseases and may cause disruption in both the male and female reproductive systems.

There are many unknowns – possible physical and psychological damage; the relationship between cannabis abuse and crime; perhaps most important, whether cannabis leads to the abuse of more serious drugs. As a result, it is not thought sensible to relax the current controls on cannabis.

SLANG NAMES Some of the common slang terms for cannabis, in its various forms, are:

Afghan (black)	Hashish	Shit
Charas	Hash oil	Smoke
Charge	Hay	Sticks
Chitari	Indian hemp	Stuff
Dagga	Kief	Takrouri
Dope	Kif	Tea
Ganga	Loco weed	Temple balls
Ganja	Marijuana	Weed
Grass	Mary	
Hash	Pot	

CANNABIS

Drugs	Class	Medical uses	Dependence potential		Duration of effect (in hours)	Methods of administration licit and illicit	Possible effects[1]	Possible effects of overdose[1]	Possible withdrawal symptoms	Medical preparation in which individual drugs occur
			Physical	Psycho-logical						
Herbal	B	–	Degree unknown	Moderate	2 to 4	Oral, smoked	Euphoria, relaxed inhibitions, increased appetite, disorientated behaviour	Fatigue, paranoia, possible psychosis	Insomnia, hyperactivity and decreased appetite reported in a limited number of individuals	–
Resin	B	–	Degree unknown	Moderate	2 to 4	Oral, smoked				–
Oil	B	–	Degree unknown	Moderate	2 to 4	Oral, smoked				–

Note: Tolerance: Yes — with continued heavy use (for Herbal, Resin, and Oil).

[1] The effects of individual drugs may be enhanced when taken with alcohol or in combination with other drugs.

SOLVENTS AND VOLATILE SUBSTANCES

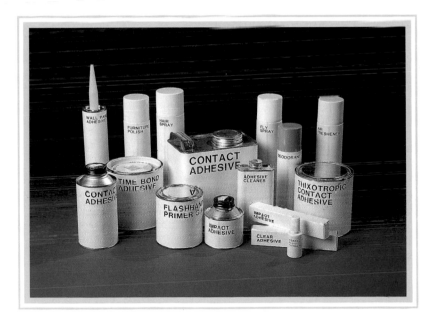

SOLVENTS AND VOLATILE SUBSTANCES

GENERAL DESCRIPTION

The increase in solvent abuse is a recent phenomenon, particularly worrying because it affects young children and can quickly lead to severe psychological dependence.

The popular term 'glue-sniffing' is too restrictive as the problem covers the inhalation of many household substances, from paint, to lighter fuel, to hair spray. For this reason it would be more accurate to refer to it generally as solvent or volatile substance abuse. It has been estimated that an average household will have about 30 substances that could be abused.

Common effects include drunken and anti-social behaviour. Though usually just a passing phase of youthful experimentation or group fashion, misuse of solvents can cause serious problems and accidental deaths.

HISTORY In ancient Greece, the Priestess at the Oracle of Delphi inhaled fumes (probably carbon dioxide) from crevices in the rocks so that her 'visions' could assist the making of prophecies. In Hebrew and Judaic times people inhaled the vapours from perfumes, ointment and burning spices as part of their religious ceremonies.

Laughing gas (nitrous oxide) was produced in the late 1800s and was soon used as a recreational drug because of its euphoric effect. Chloroform and ether were later similarly taken to produce intoxication. These are all precursors of our problems today.

Solvent abuse as we know it clearly emerged during the 1950s in the USA, and has since spread throughout the world, including the United Kingdom.

SUBSTANCES ABUSED Many products in general use, both domestic and industrial, are inhaled for the intoxication they bring. Commonly misused are:

- Fast drying glues, cements and contact adhesives.
- Paints, lacquers, thinners, paint and plaster removers, and correcting fluid and thinner.
- Petroleum products, lighter fuel (including butane gas), anti-freeze, dry-cleaning fluids, hair lacquer and nail varnish remover.
- Propellant gases in aerosol sprays including anti-perspirant and deodorant, air freshener, fly spray, paint spray, hair spray and fire extinguishers.
- Surgical spirit, shoe and metal cleaners and polish, and dyes.

No list can be exhaustive as new substances are being found and experimented with all the time. Any item containing one of the following chemicals may be abused:

acetate

benzene

carbon tetrachloride

chloroform

cyclotexane

ethyl ether and various
  alcohols

ketones including acetone

mexane

naptha

perchlorethylene

toluene

trichlorethylene

trichlorophane

HOW SOLVENTS ARE TAKEN Because there is such a wide range of products misued, several techniques are used to inhale the vapours from them.

The most common is direct sniffing. To enhance the effects of the vapour by increasing its concentration, glue and similar substances are generally sniffed from plastic sandwich, freezer or crisp bags. The bag is placed over the face and the fumes breathed in until intoxication is achieved. A polythene bag such as a bin-liner is sometimes used which completely covers the head and shoulders.

Thinners and other similar substances may be sniffed from a saturated cloth, rag or coat sleeve.

WHO MISUSES SOLVENTS? The vast majority of misusers are between the ages of 11 and 16 although some much older users also come to notice.

Currently there is a larger proportion of boys than girls involved.

They may come from any social background although children from inner-city areas are more likely to be drawn into this type of behaviour.

Misuse often takes place in groups. It may occur in the home, in school, in the street, on waste ground and in derelict and deserted buildings.

DANGERS There are grave dangers involved in solvent misuse which may result in death or cause long-term damage to health.

Misuse may bring on an adverse or even fatal heart condition. This is more likely if the user is over-exerted either during or immediately after misuse.

Spraying butane gas or aerosols into the mouth may affect the throat tissues making them swell and causing asphyxiation.

Manufacturers do change the chemical formulation of their products which makes it difficult to assess the dangers involved. Often these products contain poisonous substances.

Users may heat the product over a fire or other naked heat source to increase the concentration of the vapours. Some may even smoke whilst misusing. In either case there is a serious risk of fire as many of the products are inflammable.

Misuse often occurs in isolated places or in dangerous environments. This adds to the risk as intoxicated individuals may not be able to look after themselves properly or obtain help.

Combining solvent misuse with other drugs such as alcohol greatly increases the dangers involved.

EFFECTS Users become intoxicated on solvents more quickly than with alcohol because the substances enter the bloodstream from the lungs instead of the stomach. The immediate effects may take the user by surprise as rapid intoxication sets in. There will be a dazed, unsteady appearance and behaviour, vacant stare, indistinct, slurred speech and visual disturbance.

Some users experience hallucinations. They may respond by becoming aggressive and committing reckless and bizarre acts.

Occasionally they will continue into serious intoxication, when they are likely to be unaware of everyday hazards and at risk from accidents. Finally they may become drowsy or unconscious. This brings the danger of vomiting and choking. Any of these risk situations can give rise to accidental death.

Long-term or chronic use may lead to a permanent 'sniffer's rash' around the nose and mouth, conjunctivitis, liver and kidney damage, cardiac irregularities and in extreme cases brain damage.

Some people are more vulnerable than others to these harmful effects but young and inexperienced users run the greatest risks. Children have died the first time they have experimented with these substances.

During the 1980s there were about 405 solvent misuse related deaths. Currently there are over 100 deaths each year from this cause. Of the 112 deaths in 1990, 83 per cent involved persons under the age of 20.

Not only are more young people dying each year but research indicates that there is also a significant upward trend in the more dangerous forms of misuse. Whilst during the early part of the 1980s the use of gas fuels and pressurised aerosols accounted for less than 40 per cent of solvent misuse deaths, this rose to almost 75 per cent in 1988.

There is no evidence of significant physical dependence. But psychological dependence can develop, and some find it extremely hard to break the habit.

RECOGNISING SOLVENT ABUSE There are several tell-tale signs which suggest possible solvent abuse:

- Drunken behaviour.
- Rowdy and silly behaviour, and uncontrolled giggling.
- Self-inflicted injuries and accidents.
- Anti-social behaviour, including violence, aggressiveness and dishonesty.
- Unusual spots, marks or rings around mouth and nose.
- Red eyes or heightened facial colouring.
- Chemical smell on breath.
- Glue or solvent stains on clothing.
- Possession of plastic bags and solvents.
- General decline in performance, especially at school.
- Truanting.
- Change in personality and mental confusion.
- Altered friendship patterns.

CONTROLS Solvent misuse is not in itself a criminal offence, although the police are often the first to be called when the problem arises. Essentially it is a social problem requiring a multi-agency approach, with the police working in liaison with the other caring agencies involved, including the social, probation, medical and education services.

Most sniffers are adolescents who start off experimenting, much as children often try smoking. For this reason the criminal law is not considered the most appropriate response.

However, the criminal law may be invoked to deal with the results of solvent misuse, such as criminal damage, assaults and offences of disorder and nuisance. Where the evidence does not amount to a specific offence, the person may still be liable to arrest and be bound over to keep the peace.

In less serious cases, when other offences are not involved, it may only be necessary for the parents to be informed of the circumstances by the police or another agency. If abuse is persistent, the juvenile could, under the Children Act 1989, be dealt with as being in need of care and control. Such action is rare and would be taken in consultation with other caring agencies.

Shop owners, managers and staff need to be especially aware of the problem and symptoms of solvent abuse. They should make a determined effort to prevent the unwise sale of these substances and constantly supervise DIY areas in shops. Vigilance is required when groups of teenagers gather together by the relevant counters as sniffers often steal.

Retailers who want help or advice can contact their local police or social services department. Many local Chambers of Trade also run successful 'early warning systems' to combat the problem.

The organisation Re-Solv (see page 171) publishes a useful booklet 'Solvent and Volatile Substance Abuse – Retail Training' specifically to assist retailers.

The Intoxicating Substances (Supply) Act 1985 prohibits the supply of solvents to people under 18, when the supplier knows or has reasonable cause to believe the substance is likely to be used for the purpose of intoxication.

MISCELLANEOUS DRUGS

MISCELLANEOUS DRUGS

This section covers a number of different types of drugs which are misused for a variety of reasons. They include:

- *DRUGS IN SPORT* – Drugs that are misused in connection with sporting activities, in particular anabolic steroids.
- *OVER-THE-COUNTER DRUGS (OTC)* – A group of drugs which can be purchased without prescription in a pharmacy. Some may be purchased in ordinary retail shops and are used to treat minor everyday ailments.
- *LAXATIVES.*
- *ALKYL NITRITES* – The misuse of these is predominantly restricted to the gay community.

Other than over-the-counter drugs these drugs generally fall outside the groups covered in the rest of the book.

DRUGS IN SPORT

Concern has been growing for some time in this country regarding the use of drugs, including anabolic steroids, by sportspeople to enhance their performance. The Government is particularly anxious to protect young athletes against unscrupulous coaches who supply drugs for such purposes.

This section is intended as a general briefing for parents and others who may suspect that children and young people in their charge are taking substances in connection with their sporting activities. Details of organisations which may assist further are shown on page 173.

HISTORY The use of drugs by sportspeople is not a new development. It has a long history although misuse did not become widespread until after 1945.

The use of steroids initially appeared to be restricted to field events and to throwers in particular, whilst any misuse by track athletes tended to involve stimulants.

Although the practice obviously gave those athletes an unfair advantage and was regarded as cheating, it was not until 1967 that the International Olympic Committee (IOC) first banned some types of drugs. Testing for drugs was not introduced until the Olympic Games in Munich five years later.

The list of substances now banned by sporting authorities numbers about 3,700 and comprises:

ANALGESICS – The misuse and effects of these drugs have been covered in the section starting on page 28.

Competitors may use analgesics to decrease the amount of pain suffered from injury or illness. In addition to the psychological and physical dependence which may follow with continuous use, it enables a sportsperson to mask his injuries and increase his pain threshold. This may lead to further or permanent damage.

Analgesic substances are contained in cold and other remedial treatments which are available without prescription over the counter.

STIMULANTS – The misuse and effects of these drugs have also been covered in the appropriate section in this book starting on page 75.

Stimulants are used by competitors to increase alertness, reduce fatigue, increase competitiveness and hostility. They produce a psychological and physical stimulus which may give a competitor unfair advantage.

Several competitors have died after using stimulants. When a sportsperson exercises vigorously, for a long period of time or in a warm environment, the body overheats and the effects of the drug make it difficult for the body to cool down. This leads to dehydration and decreased circulation. The resulting adverse effects on the heart and other organs can be fatal.

Many stimulant substances are present in cough and cold medications such as decongestants which are available without a prescription over the counter.

BETA-BLOCKERS – These drugs are used medically to treat certain heart conditions including heart disease, high blood pressure and heart rate. They may be misused in particular sports where a steady hand and accuracy is required such as in shooting, archery and snooker. The action of the drugs on the heart and blood vessels is to reduce tremor that may be induced by the tension, nervousness and anxiety of the occasion.

Low blood pressure, slow heart rate and fatigue may be experienced by a person without a heart problem who misuses beta-blockers. The heart may even stop because it has been slowed down too much.

The IOC Medical Commission will advise sportspeople on alternative acceptable preparations that can be used whilst participating in sports to treat heart-related problems.

DIURETICS – These are drugs which help to remove fluids from the body. They are used medically to treat fluid retention in diseases of the heart, kidney and liver, and in pre-menstrual tension.

They are misused in sport as a masking agent to prevent detection of other drugs. They do so by increasing output of urine thereby lowering the concentration of drugs in the body and making detection more difficult. They are also used to reduce weight quickly in sports involving weight categories.

There is a serious health risk involved in misusing diuretics. The body requires a considerable intake of fluid before, during and after exercise. Losing too much water will result in dehydration causing faintness and dizziness, muscle cramps, headaches and nausea. Damage to the kidneys and heart is possible which could result in death.

ANABOLIC STEROIDS – These are covered in detail below.

POLYPEPTIDE HORMONES – These drugs have an effect similar to that of anabolic steroids. Competitors misuse these substances to stimulate the production of naturally occurring steroids, muscle growth and the repair of body tissue.

Partial restrictions are placed on alcohol, cannabis, local anaesthetics and corticosteroids (a drug which has anti-inflammatory action on injured joints thereby reducing discomfort, stiffness and pain).

As a general rule the object is to ban those substances which enhance performance but not those which allow an athlete to compete by treating or relieving some existing adverse medical condition. Anomalies arise where a substance may have both characteristics e.g. a cold remedy which is also a stimulant.

Beta-blockers may be misused by sportspeople who require a steady hand, but alcohol may also be used for the same purpose and is not completely banned.

Great Britain has taken a strong stance in attempting to rid sport of drug misuse. It was one of the leading countries to introduce drug testing and, in particular, out of season testing. Initially sports governing bodies were encouraged by the British Sports Council to implement anti-drug measures. In 1984 they were required to do so under threat that grants and services would be withheld until effective steps were taken.

ANABOLIC STEROIDS

WHAT ARE ANABOLIC STEROIDS? Steroidal hormones are produced naturally in the male and female sex organs, the adrenal cortex and the placenta. The respective hormones have distinct roles in the reproductive physiologies of the male and female.

The hormones in the male, including the important testosterone, affect the body in two particular ways. Firstly, they are responsible for the growth and functioning of the male sex organs and the 'masculinising' or 'virilising' effects of male development. These effects are known as **androgenic** and the male sex hormones are known as androgens. Secondly, they assist the development of muscle tissue which result in a 'building up' or **anabolic** effect on the body.

Hormones vary in these effects although testosterone is clearly one which is more androgenic than anabolic. The majority of synthetic anabolic steroids are derived from the basic steroid structure of the naturally occurring testosterone although manufacturers make efforts to increase the anabolic and reduce the androgenic effects. So far, a steroid with only anabolic action has not yet been developed and so they will all have some virilising side-effects.

MEDICAL USE Anabolic steroids have been used in the treatment of anaemic conditions, wasting and bone diseases and breast cancer. They are also used as a replacement therapy in men deficient in the naturally occurring male hormones.

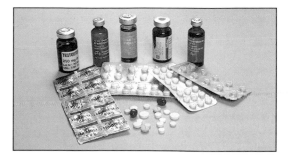

The range of anabolic steroids produced in the form of tablets, capsules, injections and creams is enormous. It would be almost impossible to identify all relevant preparations

Side-effects may occur, particularly when the drug is taken long term.

CONTROLS ON ANABOLIC STEROIDS Anabolic steroids are classified as prescription-only medicines under the Medicines Act 1968. They may be legally supplied to the public only on prescription issued by a doctor. It is not an offence to possess anabolic steroids for personal use although supplying without a prescription could result in prosecution. Importing them into the country for personal use is not illegal and this is undoubtedly the source for supplies of these drugs which are distributed to members of sports and health clubs.

The legal position of anabolic steroids was considered by the Advisory Council on the Misuse of Drugs. Although there were strong views to the contrary, the Council advised against bringing these drugs within the control of the Misuse of Drugs Act 1971.

The Government is following the Advisory Council's recommendation and, instead of legislation, proposes a 'carefully targeted package of measures' to deal with the current problem. This may include legislative provisions but only to make it illegal to supply anabolic steroids and similar named substances to minors i.e. those under 18 years of age, with or without payment. The provision is specially aimed at the coach who supplies steroids to young sportspeople for whom he has responsibility. The legislation would include all anabolic steroids, together with a small number of polypeptide hormones (chemical chains of amino acids which promote the action of other hormones).

This is a complicated subject and there is some contention whether or not a preparation falls into a particular category. However, it is proposed that anabolic steroids would be defined generically and supported by an up-to-date list of named drugs. Omission from the list would not mean that an anabolic steroid is not covered. The suggested list would include the following:

Anabolic steroids

Atamestane	Methenolone
Bolandiol	Metribolone
Bolasterone	Mibolerone
Bolazine	Nandrolone
Boldenone	Norboletone
Bolenol	Norclostebol
Bolmantalate	Norethandrolone
Clostebol acetate	Ovandrotone

Drostanolone
Enestebol
Epitiostanol
Epostane
Ethyloestranol
Flumedroxone
Fluoxymesterone
Formebolone
Furazabol
Mebolazine
Mepitiostane
Mesabolone
Mestanolone
Methandriol
Methandienone

Oxabolone
Oxandrolone
Oxymesterone
Oxymetholone
Propetandrol
Quinbolone
Roxibolone
Silandrone
Stanolone
Stanozolol
Stenbolone
Thiomesterone
Tibolone
Trenbolone
Triolostane

Androgenic steroids

Mesterolone
Methyltestosterone

Oral Turinabol
Testosterone

A generic definition of polypeptide hormones is not possible and those subject to the new provisions would be specifically named. The suggested list is as follows:

Polypeptide hormones

Gonadorelin
Human chorionic gonado-
    trophin

Somatrem

Somatropin

Other elements of the package include:

- Enhanced educational efforts aimed at the public and at sport in particular.
- Additional research into the extent of steroid misuse.
- Research into improved testing and detection methods for use in sport.
- More vigorous action under existing legislation against those advertising steroids for sale.

EFFECTS Why do healthy sportspeople use anabolic steroids? If taken in conjunction with a rigorous training programme and a good diet, anabolic steroids increase the body's protein production which results in greater muscle bulk and therefore strength. They allow the user to train harder and recover more quickly. To improve their competitiveness some users also seek the increased aggression which can be a side-effect particularly associated with the male-sex type hormone.

DANGERS The dangers involved in using anabolic steroids have yet to be fully established although initial claims based on limited data are alarming.

It is stated that prolonged use may cause high blood pressure and cholesterol levels leading to heart disease; liver damage including jaundice, tumours, bleeding into the liver, and liver failure; impairment of bone growth; and mental disorders including paranoia.

Increased aggression and sexual appetite have been reported in men and women. But with repeated use of steroids, sterility and impotence in men may follow. This may also be accompanied by a shrinking and hardening of the testicles and breast development.

In women, changes in the sex organs may be experienced too, accompanied by a disruption in the menstrual cycle. The development of masculine characteristics such as facial hair, acne and a deepening voice may also occur. Some of these changes may be irreversible even when the use of steroids has ceased.

Steroid use may seriously damage the unborn child, particularly during early pregnancy. In children and young people it may affect growth and lead to stunting.

Although not thought to be physically addictive, some users become psychologically dependent on steroids believing that their level of physical and sporting performance will drop without them. This may be accompanied by lethargy and depression.

The body's defences against physical stress and over-exertion are also suppressed by the drug, resulting in overheating or extreme fatigue. This condition, as well as an overdose of steroids have proved fatal.

Although misuse of steroids is considered a different form of drug misuse to that described in the rest of the book, there are many similar dangers e.g. the transmission of life-threatening infections such as HIV if contaminated hypodermic syringes are shared between users. The inherent dangers associated with black market drugs apply equally to steroids if the proprietary origin and make-up of the drugs are not known.

These substances are increasingly available and misuse is not restricted to national or international sporting events. No sport is immune but some sporting events such as weightlifting and body-building are more susceptible than others.

The Government recognises that more research is required into this aspect of drug misuse. However, the warning signs are already clear enough. Parents, teachers and others who supervise children and young people involved in sporting activities should be conscious of this developing situation and be on their guard.

OVER-THE-COUNTER (OTC) DRUGS

Over-the-counter (OTC) drugs consist of a wide range of preparations which can be obtained without a prescription. They are either pharmacy medicines which can only be sold at a registered pharmacy under the supervision of a pharmacist or medicines on the general sales list which do not require supervision and can be sold in shops which are not registered pharmacies.

It would be impracticable to produce a comprehensive list of all the brand name preparations that are liable to misuse. They do, however, fall into specific groups of drugs and the following information will hopefully be sufficient to help the reader to be aware of the problem and, if necessary, enquire further. The OTC drug groups of concern are:

ANTIHISTAMINES

These are drugs which prevent or diminish the effects of histamine – a chemical substance released by the body tissues in allergic reactions which cause irritation.

MEDICAL USE Antihistamines are used to treat nasal allergies, particularly hayfever, irritative running nose, sneezing, allergic rashes, pruritus, insect bites and stings and also drug allergies.

They are used in cough preparations and medicines for colds and flu. Some have an effective anti-emetic action and are used to prevent travel sickness, vertigo and other causes of nausea, including middle ear disorders.

EFFECTS Many antihistamines cause sedation although they vary significantly in effect from slight drowsiness to deep sleep. Some are fairly short acting whilst others may last up to 12 hours.

Some newer types of antihistamines have less of a sedating effect. In most cases there may be some degree of dizziness and lack of co-ordination which may affect performance of skilled tasks such as driving a motor vehicle or operating powered machinery. The effects will be greatly enhanced if alcohol is also consumed.

A whole range of other side-effects have been reported which vary quite considerably depending on the drug used and the individual. These may include headache, blurred vision, nausea, vomiting, diarrhoea or constipation and low blood pressure.

The user may also feel depressed although with high doses quite opposite symptoms of stimulation may appear. In exceptional circumstances, these may develop into a more serious condition.

A vast quantity of these drugs are taken each year, particularly in early summer. Used according to the manufacturers' directions, countless individuals obtain relief without adverse effects.

ABUSE There are many preparations on the market containing different types of antihistamine drugs. Not all are misused although many have that potential. The misuse of cyclizine has particularly come to notice in recent times. Some users apparently mix the drug with heroin or methadone in an attempt to produce a substance similar to Diconal (page 50). One of the important side-effects of opiate analgesics is that they produce nausea and a way of getting over this is to combine them with an anti-emetic.

Cyclizine is produced in a white scored tablet containing 50mg of cyclizine hydrochloride marked 'WELLCOME T4A' under the brand name Valoid. It also appears as an injection in 1ml ampoules.

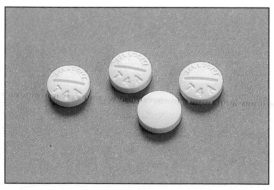

Valoid tablets contain 50mg of the drug cyclizine hydrochloride — an antihistamine

 Actual size of Valoid tablets

SYMPATHOMIMETICS

These are drugs which have the ability to produce physiological changes similar to those caused by the action of the sympathetic nervous system.

MEDICAL USE Sympathomimetics are used either as vasoconstricters or vasodilators in the treatment of hypotension and serious heart conditions, and as bronchodilators in asthma and similar conditions. The major sympathomimetics in general OTC use are those in cold preparations to 'dry-up' runny noses and ease chestiness, and as nasal decongestants.

EFFECTS Although they are not related to the antihistamines and exert their actions by an entirely different pharmacological mechanism, the effects of sympathomimetics are in many ways similar to antihistamines.

A number are structurally similar to amphetamines e.g. ephedrine (see page 91), pseudoephedrine and phenylpropanolamine. Medical use may result in central nervous system stimulation. Misuse is intended to achieve feelings of stimulation and euphoria similar to that obtained from amphetamines.

OPIATES

MEDICAL USE There are many medicinal preparations which may be purchased over the counter of a pharmacy which contain low concentrations of opiates, particularly morphine and codeine. Although both are controlled drugs, Schedule 5 of the Misuse of Drugs Regulations exempts them from virtually all controlled drug requirements (see page 18).

Low doses of codeine are used in analgesic preparations for headaches, etc. and as a cough suppressant in various linctuses. Low concentrations of morphine are contained in some diarrhoea treatments.

ABUSE AND EFFECTS The misuse of opiates have been dealt with in detail in the section on analgesics. The information relating to effects, dangers and dependence apply to these products. They are intended to be used for medicinal purposes and taken in accordance with the recommended dose.

If misused in frequent and excessive amounts, the harm to the body could be significant. Chronic analgesic abuse has led to serious kidney failure, peptic ulceration, gastro-intestinal bleeding, anaemia and psychiatric disturbances.

As codeine is often combined with paracetamol, misuse carries a high degree of risk, as paracetamol is very toxic to the liver, even in modest overdose.

LAXATIVES

MEDICAL USE Laxatives or purgatives are taken for the relief of constipation. There are a number of proprietary brands which can be purchased over the counter.

EFFECTS The abuse of laxatives may result in a decrease in the sensitivity of the mucous membranes of the intestines so that larger doses are required, tolerance develops and the natural processes cease to function without the drug.

Prolonged use may result in diarrhoea, loss of important body salts, muscular weakness and weight loss. Unchecked it could soon develop into a very serious medical condition.

Young women, from the start of their early teens, may abuse laxatives which leads to, or is already part of, a condition known as anorexia nervosa. It is a pathological condition which is believed to be psychological in origin. It starts with a distaste for, or phobia about, fatness and develops into loss of appetite and a refusal or inability to eat. This is often exacerbated by the taking of laxatives.

If the condition is not reversed it may result in emaciation, cessation of menstruation, other serious disorders and eventually death.

ALKYL NITRITES

There are a number of compounds within the alkyl nitrite group including amyl, butyl and isobutyl nitrites.

USES The nitrites have been used in industry for various reasons ranging from preserving food to the production of perfume. They are powerful oxidising agents and highly flammable.

Amyl nitrite, discovered in 1852, is a clear yellow liquid with a fragrant odour and pungent aromatic taste. It has been used medically since 1867 in the treatment of angina pectoris (heart-related chest pains). There is now a whole range of medical preparations for this condition and the use of amyl nitrite is restricted to the emergency treatment of angina attacks when instant relief is necessary.

Absorbed through the mucous membranes of the lungs it is the quickest acting of all of the nitrites – the effects being evident within 10 seconds. It causes the walls of blood vessels to relax and this is most apparent in the head and neck. Within 30 to 40 seconds the face flushes, the head and neck perspire and the heart rate increases. The heart valves open up increasing the flow of blood and oxygen to areas of the heart muscle which were deficient, thereby providing the necessary relief to the angina sufferer. The action of the drug usually only lasts about five minutes.

A second use is as an antidote for cyanide poisoning. The drug is held for emergency use in hospitals and places where there is a possible risk of poisoning in factories and laboratories.

ABUSE The misuse of amyl nitrite and the other nitrites may cause a brief 'high' which produces pleasant perceptual distortions. It is also alleged to intensify sexual experiences, both homosexual and heterosexual.

AVAILABILITY The medical preparation containing amyl nitrite is not as readily available as it has been in recent years and abuse is therefore not as prevalent. The current source for non-medicinal alkyl nitrites is mainly through mail order, sex shops and gay bars.

Alkyl nitrites have been produced in the USA and imported into this country as room deodorisers. They are sold in small brown bottles similar to eye-dropper bottles, as well as other more commercial looking containers. They are marketed under a number of colourful names which suggest other uses!

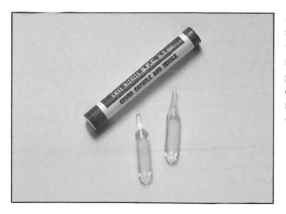

Amyl nitrite is produced in a small glass vial protected by wadding and an outer reinforced paper tube. The glass vial or vitrellae is made of very thin glass. To use, the tube is crushed and the vapours inhaled

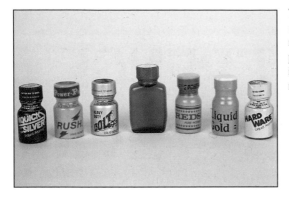

The main source of alkyl nitrites for non-medical use is not from pharmaceutical preparations but from supplies imported into the country and marketed as room-deodorisers

EFFECTS The main side-effects of using alkyl nitrites may include light-headedness, weakness, headaches (both short-term and pro-longed throbbing headaches) and flushing of the face and neck.

Larger doses and long-term use may cause nausea, dizziness, delirium, decreased heart rate, impaired respiration, low blood pressure and fainting.

Both psychological dependence and tolerance may develop.

SLANG NAMES

Nitrates	Bananas
Poppers	Rush
Snappers	

REFERENCE
SECTION

DRUG STATISTICS

The drug statistics, which relate to the situation in the UK, have been taken from the Home Office statistical bulletin (issues no 19 and 6 published on 13 September 1991 and 19 March 1992 respectively) with information being reproduced from selected years 1981, 1985, 1988 to 1990 inclusively (referred to below as 'the selected years'). Tables K, L and O also include information for 1991.

Using 1981 as the base line they show developing trends over the last decade with a mid-term indicator at 1985 and more pertinent information from the three most recent annual reports.

NUMBER AND QUANTITY OF SEIZURES OF CONTROLLED DRUGS

The total number of seizures of all drugs has been increasing annually since 1981. Between 1985 and 1990 the overall number of seizures doubled, reaching a total of almost 60,900. Most of the seizures (87 per cent) involved Class B drugs – in the main cannabis. These may have been alone or with Class A or C drugs.

It would be totally misleading to compare the quantities of individual drugs seized to establish which is the most serious problem without considering the relative bulk and the relative harmfulness of the different substances. One kilogram of heroin is infinitely more dangerous than one kilogram of cannabis. These statistics should be used only to indicate individual drug trends.

---

[1] As a seizure can involve more than one drug, figures for individual drugs cannot be added together to produce totals.
[2] Drugs are seized in a variety of forms but where possible they have been converted to weights.
[3] Includes 316 crack seizures.
[4] Includes 766 MDMA (ecstasy) seizures.
[5] Includes 399 MDMA (ecstasy) seizures.

Table A shows the number of seizures[1] of Class A drugs by drug type for the selected years.

TABLE A	NUMBER OF SEIZURES				
Drug type	1981	1985	1988	1989	1990
Cocaine	503	662	829	2,045	1,805[3]
Dextromoramide	80	53	25	37	29
Dipipanone	370	92	49	59	52
Heroin	819	3,176	2,197	2,728	2,593
LSD	384	494	361	967	1,859
Methadone	402	452	209	444	362
Morphine	243	135	96	136	143
Opium	137	52	32	41	47
Pethidine	135	90	41	51	31
Other Class A	119	135	248	1,015[4]	734[5]
All Class A	2,513	4,899	3,873	6,915	7,153

Table B shows the quantity[2] of seizures of Class A drugs by drug type for the selected years.

TABLE B	QUANTITY OF SEIZURES (KILOGRAMS)				
Drug type	1981	1985	1988	1989	1990
Cocaine	21.1	85.4	323.2	498.8	611.0
Dextromoramide	0.022	0.009	0.004	0.016	0.008
Dipipanone	0.011	0.013	0.014	0.004	0.001
Heroin	93.4	366.4	235.7	351.4	602.7
LSD	0.024	0.010	0.016	0.023	0.040
Methadone	0.953	0.144	0.072	0.482	0.273
Morphine	6.5	0.1	0.1	4.1	20.8
Opium	16.5	2.5	4.0	2.2	7.6
Pethidine	0.3	0.2	—	0.1	0.1
Other Class A	0.6	0.6	4.4	6.3	14.9

Although the actual number of seizures of heroin and cocaine decreased in 1990, the quantities seized reached record levels of over 600 kilograms for each drug. The rise in the number of LSD seizures in recent years should also be noted. Between 1989 and 1990 they almost doubled to just under 2,000.

Table C shows the number of seizures[1] of Class B and C drugs by drug type for the selected years.

TABLE C NUMBER OF SEIZURES					
Drug type	1981	1985	1988	1989	1990
Class B drugs					
Amphetamines	1,117	3,471	3,277	3,322	4,629
Barbiturates[3]	–	146	92	128	74
Cannabis (herbal)	8,500	10,388	9,550	7,497	7,121
Cannabis plants	1,787	1,594	641	806	818
Cannabis resin	8,911	14,991	24,126	38,400	46,769
Cannabis liquid	254	142	145	125	126
Methaqualone[4]	–	33	15	11	3
Other Class B	229	52	59	100	118
All Class B	**17,953**	**26,928**	**35,266**	**46,984**	**55,634**
Class C drugs					
Methaqualone[i]	143	–	–	–	–
Other Class C	11	73	212	492	802
All Class C	**152**	**73**	**212**	**492**	**802**

Table D shows the quantity[2] of seizures of Class B and C drugs by drug type for the selected years.

TABLE D	QUANTITY OF SEIZURES (KILOGRAMS)				
Drug type	1981	1985	1988	1989	1990
Class B drugs					
Amphetamines	18.1	76.6	137.1	108.2	303.8
Barbiturates[3]	–	1.1	786.7	6.3	1.1
Cannabis (herbal)	16,874.4	14,281.8	24,098.1	6,780.9	9,337.5
Cannabis plants[5]	21,178.0	16,092.0	4,762.0	6,263.0	34,299.0
Cannabis resin	7,817.5	7,861.2	21,364.9	52,577.9	21,549.5
Cannabis liquid	81.6	21.8	12.8	10.4	1.6
Methaqualone[4]	–	0.1	–	2.1	0.1
Other Class B	0.2	0.1	0.1	0.1	0.2
Class C drugs					
Methaqualone[4]	1.2	–	–	–	–
Other Class C	0.005	0.362	0.393	1.066	1.317

[1] As a seizure can involve more than one drug, figures for individual drugs cannot be added together to produce totals.
[2] Drugs are seized in a variety of forms but where possible they have been converted to weights.
[3] Barbiturates were brought under control with effect from 1 January 1985.
[4] Methaqualone was changed from a Class C drug to a Class B drug with effect from 1 January 1985.
[5] Number of plants.

Not only did the number of seizures of amphetamine increase significantly (40 per cent) in 1990 but the quantity seized showed almost a 300 per cent increase. Quantities of cannabis seized fell in 1990 against an increasing number of seizures.

Table E shows the number and percentage of seizures[1] of controlled drugs divided into Classes A, B and C for the selected years.

TABLE E NUMBER AND PERCENTAGE OF SEIZURES	1981	1985	1988	1989	1990
NUMBER OF SEIZURES					
Class A drugs	2,513	4,899	3,873	6,915	7,153
Class B drugs	17,953	26,928	35,266	46,984	55,634
Class C drugs	152	73	212	492	802
All drugs	19,428	30,466	38,235	52,131	60,859
PERCENTAGE OF SEIZURES					
Class A drugs	12.9	16.1	10.1	13.3	11.8
Class B drugs	92.4	88.4	92.2	90.1	91.4
Class C drugs	0.8	0.2	0.6	0.9	1.3
All drugs	100	100	100	100	100

[1] As a seizure can involve more than one drug, figures for individual drug classes cannot be added together to produce totals.

OFFENDERS FOUND GUILTY, CAUTIONED OR DEALT WITH BY COMPOUNDING

SERIOUSNESS OF THE OFFENCE The offence categories have been divided into unlawful possession and trafficking. Trafficking includes the unlawful acts of production of drugs (other than cannabis), supply, possession with intent to supply, and importing and exporting.

Table F shows the number and percentages of people found guilty, cautioned or dealt with by compounding for offences of unlawful possession and trafficking for the selected years.

TABLE F	NUMBER OF PEOPLE				
People found guilty, cautioned or dealt with by compounding	1981	1985	1988	1989	1990
Total	17,921	26,958	30,515	38,415	44,922
of whom:					
Unlawful possession	14,850	22,569	26,372	33,207	39,350
Trafficking	2,865	5,244	5,019	6,108	6,680

In 1990, following the similar trend of previous years, 88 per cent of the cases were for unlawful possession and the majority of these (92 per cent) were for offences involving cannabis.

TYPES OF DISPOSAL

Table G shows the number of people found guilty and sentenced by a court to (i) an immediate custody sentence and (ii) a fine, cautioned or dealt with by compounding for the selected years.

TABLE G	NUMBER OF PEOPLE				
	1981	1985	1988	1989	1990
Sentenced by a court	17,667	22,972	20,962	21,972	26,713
to include:					
(i) immediate imprisonment	1,931	4,535	3,523	3,855	3,402
(ii) fine	11,656	12,985	12,523	15,533	16,437
Cautioned	254	3,624	8,820	12,380	17,025
Settled by compounding	—	362	733	1,063	1,184

These statistics clearly show the Government's policy of encouraging the use of cautioning in lieu of prosecution. 1990 saw more individuals being cautioned (40 per cent) than fined (35 per cent). Fewer than 10 per cent of offenders were sentenced to an immediate term of custody.

TYPE OF OFFENCE

Table H shows the number of people[1] found guilty, cautioned or dealt with by compounding for drugs offences by drug type for the selected years.

TABLE H	NUMBER OF PEOPLE				
Drug type	1981	1985	1988	1989	1990
Cocaine	566	632	591	786	860
Dipipanone	498	97	44	44	37
Heroin	808	3,227	1,856	1,769	1,605
LSD	345	539	240	435	915
Methadone	445	413	162	172	154
Amphetamines	1,074	2,946	2,538	2,395	2,330
Cannabis	15,388	21,337	26,111	33,669	40,194
Other	1,141	1,023	1,222	1,263	1,670
All drugs	17,921	26,958	30,515	38,415	44,922

[1] As the same person may be found guilty, cautioned or dealt with by compounding for offences involving more than one drug, rows cannot be added together to produce sub-totals or totals.

AGE OF OFFENDERS

Table J shows the number and percentage of people found guilty, cautioned or dealt with by compounding for drugs offences by age for the selected years.

TABLE J NUMBER AND PERCENTAGE OF PEOPLE BY AGE					
	1981	1985	1988	1989	1990
NUMBER OF PEOPLE					
Under 17	293	827	757	1,312	2,431
17 and under 21	4,068	6,800	7,530	10,478	13,754
21 and under 25	4,886	7,425	8,964	10,564	11,856
25 and under 30	4,708	5,656	6,560	8,109	8,735
30 and over	3,966	6,250	6,974	7,952	8,146
All ages	17,921	26,958	30,515	38,415	44,922
PERCENTAGE OF PEOPLE					
Under 17	2	3	2	3	5
17 and under 21	25	25	25	27	31
21 and under 25	27	28	29	27	26
25 and under 30	26	21	21	21	19
30 and over	22	23	23	21	18
All ages	100	100	100	100	100
Average age	25.5	25.7	25.8	25.4	24.7

The number of offenders aged under 21 is on the increase and this age group is contributing significantly to the general increase in the total number of offenders. The average age of offenders has dropped to below 25 years. Current anecdotal evidence indicates that the number of people under 17 misusing drugs is far higher than indicated by these arrest and caution figures.

DRUG ADDICTION

Table K shows the number of new and renotified drug addicts reported to the Home Office for the selected years.

TABLE K		NUMBER OF ADDICTS					
Addict status	1981	1985	1988	1989	1990	1991
New drug addicts						
Total	2,248	6,409	5,212	5,639	6,923	8,007
Renotified drug addicts						
Total	–	–	7,432	9,146	10,832	12,813
All drug addicts notified						
Total	–	–	12,644	14,785	17,755	20,820

These statistics are compiled from reports made by general practitioners, police surgeons, hospitals/accident centres and prison medical officers. The method of recording these reports changed in 1986.

The number of addicts notified to the Home Office is increasing each year with the total now reaching 21,000 (1991). Included in that number were some 8,000 new addicts which represents an annual rise of 16 per cent.

Table L shows the number of new addicts[1] notified to the Home Office during the selected years, together with their drug of addiction.

TABLE L NUMBER OF NEW ADDICTS						
Drug type	1981	1985	1988	1989	1990	1991
Heroin	1,660	5,930	4,630	4,883	5,819	6,328
Methadone	431	669	576	682	1,469	2,180
Dipipanone	473	223	124	109	154	155
Cocaine	174	490	462	527	633	882
Morphine	355	326	203	259	296	185
Pethidine	45	34	44	36	39	37
Dextromoramide	59	104	80	75	78	89
Opium	–	14	18	15	14	12
Other drugs	4	8	2	1	4	1
All new addicts	2,248	6,409	5,212	5,639	6,923	8,007

[1] As an addict can be reported as addicted to more than one notifiable drug, the figures for individual drugs cannot be added together to produce totals.

Although there are 14 notifiable drugs of addiction, only those which show a significant number of cases are included in Table L. Heroin is by far the most common drug of addiction and has been throughout the last decade. The number of cocaine addicts is increasing but still only amounts to a relatively small proportion of the total. This is against a background of increasing quantities of cocaine being seized. Seizures of cocaine by weight now exceed those of heroin – over a tonne of cocaine was recovered in 1991.

Many addicts are addicted to more than one drug. In 1991, a record number of people were reported as dependent on methadone (alone or with other drugs).

DRUG ADDICT DEATHS

Table M shows the number[1] of deaths of drug addicts previously notified to the Home Office by cause during the selected years.

TABLE M		NUMBER OF DEATHS[2]			
Cause of death	1981	1985	1988	1989	1990
Not primarily associated with drug misuse	57	63 (20)	99 (14)	110 (8)	119 (6)
Natural	41	24 (15)	40 (11)	42 (8)	66 (6)
Accident	7	16 (1)	25 (1)	36	26
Homicide victim)	7	2	4	3	1
Suicide)		15 (1)	24 (1)	18	22
Unknown	2	6 (3)	6 (1)	11	4
Associated with drug misuse	83	103 (1)	179	181 (3)	206
Overdose	80	86 (1)	161	152 (1)	169
Other drug-related	3	17	13	21 (2)	22
AIDS/HIV	–	–	5	8	15
All deaths	140	166 (21)	278 (14)	291 (11)	325 (6)

[1]Excludes Northern Ireland.
[2]From 1985 onwards, addicts whose addiction arose from medical treatment are shown in brackets.

DRUG-RELATED DEATHS
Table N shows the number of drug-related deaths for the selected years.

TABLE N NUMBER OF DEATHS (PREVIOUSLY NOTIFIED ADDICTS)					
Underlying cause of death	1980	1985	1988	1989	1990
Drug dependence and non-dependent abuse of drugs	99	190	222	245	294 (86)
Deaths from poisoning					
Accidental			191	202	233 (60)
Suicide			478	433	440 (8)
Undetermined			302	279	262 (21)
AIDS		1	13	20	34 ( )
TOTAL			1,206	1,179	1,263

In 1990 there were approximately 1,300 deaths in the UK where the underlying cause was attributable to drug dependence, non-dependent abuse of drugs or controlled drugs were involved in some way.

Of the 300 deaths caused by drug dependence or non-dependent abuse of drugs, 91 involved morphine-type drugs and 112 involved misuse of volatile substances. Of the latter category, 93 were under 20 years old.

DEATHS OF REPORTED AIDS CASES

Table O shows the number of deaths of reported AIDS cases by year from 1985 to 1991.

TABLE O NUMBER OF DEATHS	1985	1986	1987	1988	1989	1990	1991
Injecting drug users							
Male	1	3	7	7	14	26	40
Female	–	1	1	6	6	8	21
All	1	4	8	13	20	34	61
All deaths							
Male	116	256	340	383	620	722	695
Female	3	10	5	23	31	35	58
All	119	266	345	406	651	757	753

Sharing contaminated syringes and needles has played an important part in the transmission of HIV infection. Because of this doctors were requested in 1987 to provide details of addicts under their care who injected drugs. Even though there had been a concerted publicity campaign warning of the dangers of injecting and sharing, in 1990 an analysis of 80 per cent of addicts revealed that two-third of these, some 9,500, were still injecting drugs.

STREET PRICES OF ILLICIT DRUGS (1991)

The police calculate the current street prices of illicit drugs from information received from street agencies, informants, prosecutions and other intelligence sources.

Prices fluctuate according to demand and availability – there are no open-market prices and drugs are worth precisely what the buyer will pay at a given time. The prices quoted can therefore only serve as a guide.

Table P shows approximate street prices of drugs.

TABLE P	DRUG PRICES	
Drug type	**per ounce**	
Heroin	£900—£1200	£50—£120 per gram
Cocaine hydrochloride	£900—£1300	£50—£100 per gram
Cocaine crack	—	£10—£30 per rock (average 0.2 grams)
LSD	—	£3—£5 per dose
Amphetamine sulphate	£90—£150	£10—£15 per gram
MDMA (ecstasy)	—	£13—£25 per dose
Cannabis (resin)	£60—£130	—
Cannabis (herbal)	£55—£100	—
Cannabis (hash oil)	—	£12—£20 per gram

WHERE TO GO FOR HELP

No matter where you live in the United Kingdom, there is always an organisation or individual that can be called upon by a user, parent, employer or any other person who requires information, advice or help. This assistance is usually no more than a local telephone call away.

A wide range of services has been established and it would be impossible to list them all here. The ones which follow are representative of those that are available. The different services can be divided into five main groups:

- NHS hospital and health centre services.
- Advisory and counselling services.
- Residential rehabilitation and treatment services.
- Self-help, parent and community groups.
- Private drug clinics.

The services that have been listed do not include the latter two categories. Information about them can be obtained from the National Organisations detailed below, many of which maintain lists of local specialist drug services, self-help, parent and community groups – too many to include in this book.

In particular, the **Standing Conference on Drug Abuse (SCODA)** maintains a comprehensive national directory of services that help drug users, their families and friends throughout the United Kingdom. The title of the publication is *Drug Problems: Where to get help* and may be found in all libraries and Citizens' Advice Bureaux. It is regularly updated and can be purchased directly from SCODA.

There is also a 'freephone' facility to obtain local contact numbers in England. Just dial 100 and ask the operator for Freephone Drug Problems.

The local telephone directories, British Telecom and Thomson's, are sources of information. If there is no service listed for your immediate areas, the nearest advisory and counselling organisation would be able to refer you to the most appropriate local agency.

Local Citizens' Advice Bureaux, the family doctor, the library and the police may provide information on advisory organisations and self-help groups in your area. Police forces are also increasingly taking part in drug referral schemes which enable people arrested to be referred to advice agencies.

Child guidance clinics and the educational welfare service can often help with drug-related problems involving school children. The social services and probation service may also be involved where there are drug problems either in school or at home. This is particularly so where there are concerns for child welfare or where a criminal offence is involved.

Employers are also becoming more aware of the existence of drug misuse in the workplace and may require assistance to develop policies to manage the problem. Details of organisations able to assist are given later in this section.

In any case of difficulty, the following national organisations can give you information about particular forms of help.

NB The information in this section has been compiled with the assistance of the Standing Conference on Drug Abuse. The inclusion of any organisation does not constitute a recommendation on the part of either SCODA or the author.

NATIONAL ORGANISATIONS

INFORMATION ABOUT LOCAL SERVICES

The Standing Conference on Drug Abuse (SCODA)
1–4 Hatton Place
Hatton Garden
London EC1N 8ND
Tel: 071 430 2341
SCODA is the national co-ordinating organisation for services for people with drugs problems.

It maintains a directory of services called *Drug Problems: where to get help* which details all the services available to drug users, their friends and families. A 'Freephone Drug Problem' facility for local contact numbers in England is also available.

The Scottish Health Education Group
Woodburn House
Cannon Lane
Edinburgh EH10 3SG
Tel: 031 447 8044
The national health education body for Scotland.

Scottish Drugs Forum
5 Oswald Street
Glasgow G1 4QR
Tel: 041 221 1175
For drugs services in Scotland.

Drugs Training Project
Department of Sociology and Social Policy
Pathfoot Building
University of Stirling
Stirling FK9 4LA
Tel: 0786 67732
Provides training and advice on drug matters for those who work with drug users and their families.

All Wales Drugs Line
1 Neville Street
Canton
Cardiff CF1 8LP
Tel: 0222 383313
For drugs services in Wales.

Welsh Committee on Drug Misuse
Secretariat
c/o HSSPIA
Welsh Office
Cathays Park
Cardiff CF1 3NQ
Tel: 0222 823925
For local drugs services and literature on drug misuse.

Health Promotion Authority for Wales
Floor 8
Brunel House
2 Fitzalan Road
Cardiff CF2 1EB
Tel: 0222 472472
For general advice on health

Northern Ireland Council for Voluntary Action
127 Ormeau Road
Belfast
BT7 1SH
Tel: 0232 321224
For drugs services in Northern Ireland.

INFORMATION AND ADVICE ABOUT HIV INFECTION AND AIDS

SCODA and Scottish Drugs Forum

SCODA and the Scottish Drugs Forum can supply information and advice about HIV and AIDS and contacts with relevant local drugs services.

Specialist Drugs Services

Most community-based specialist drugs services can advise about HIV infection and AIDS. Some operate exchange schemes for used needles and syringes.

National AIDS Helpline

The National AIDS Helpline is a free confidential advice, information and counselling service:
Tel: 0800 567 123
For free leaflets:
Tel: 0800 555 777

INFORMATION ABOUT DRUGS

The Institute for the Study of Drug Dependence (ISDD)

1–4 Hatton Place
Hatton Garden
London EC1N 8ND
Tel: 071 430 1991
The Institute publishes up-to-date material on various aspects of the use and misuse of drugs and sells publications for other organisations. A comprehensive library service is provided for interested individuals and professionals.

Teachers' Advisory Council on Alcohol and Drug Education (TACADE)

1 Hulme Place
The Crescent
Salford
Manchester M5 4QA
Tel: 061 745 8925

INFORMATION ABOUT SOLVENT AND VOLATILE SUBSTANCE MISUSE

Re-Solv

30A High Street
Stone
Staffordshire ST15 8AW
Tel: 0785 817885
Re-Solv provides general information and educational material on solvent and volatile substance misuse.

Solvent Misuse Project

National Children's Bureau
8 Wakley Street
London EC1V 7QE
Tel: 071 278 9441
Produces a directory of residential services which accept young solvent misusers.

ADVICE AND COUNSELLING

The National Association of Young People's Counselling and Advisory Services (NAYPCAS)
17–23 Albion Street
Leicester LE1 6GD
NAYPCAS can supply information about local youth counselling services – normally restricted to those under 21. Enquiries by letter only.

British Association for Counselling (BAC)
37A Sheep Street
Rugby
Warwickshire CV21 3BX
Tel: 0788 78328
BAC provides a counselling referral service on any type of problem. It will put you in touch with a local counsellor or counselling organisation.
The office is open Monday to Friday between 9am and 5pm.

The Samaritans
46 Marshal Street
London W1V 1LR
Tel: 071 734 2800
Local branches are listed in the telephone directory.
An emergency counselling service for users and families in crisis.

Release
388 Old Street
London EC1V 9LT
Tel: 071 729 9904
A national 24-hour telephone service for advice and information on legal and drug-related problems. Outside of normal working hours and at weekends use the emergency telephone number which is:
Tel: 071 603 8654

Turning Point
New Loom House
101 Back Church Lane
London E1 1LU
Tel: 071 702 2300
Turning Point can supply details of drug services available locally. It also provides a counselling service in local centres, advises companies on the development of policies and runs training courses for company personnel.

SELF-HELP GROUPS

Narcotics Anonymous
UK Service Office
PO Box 1980
London N19 3LS
Tel: 071 351 6794 (help line)
      071 351 6066 (local meetings)
For details about where the nearest Narcotics Anonymous meetings are held, or assistance to start new self-help groups for people with drugs problems.

Families Anonymous
310 Finchley Road
London NW3 7AG
Tel: 071 431 3537
Advice and support groups for families and friends of drug users. There are meetings of Families Anonymous throughout the country.

Mind
22 Harley Street
London W1
Tel: 071 637 0741
The information unit at Mind can provide details of local Mind groups which provide help for tranquilliser users and/or support for self-help groups.

Council for Involuntary Tranquilliser Problems
Cavendish House
Brighton Road
Liverpool L22 5NG
Tel: 051 525 2777
National telephone advice, information and counselling service for people with tranquilliser problems.

Aid for Addicts and Family (ADFAM)
82 Old Brompton Road
London SW7 3LQ
Tel: 071 823 9313
ADFAM provides help and support to local self-help groups countrywide and runs training courses, meetings and conferences for them. It also provides a helpline on weekdays between 10am and 5pm on the same telephone number.

DRUGS IN SPORT

The Sports Council
16 Upper Woburn Place
London
WC1H 0QP
Tel: 071 388 1277
The Sports Council can provide information on drugs in sport, drug testing and procedures.

DRUGS IN THE WORKPLACE

Department of Employment
Information 4
Caxton House
Tothill Street
London SW1H 9NF
The Department of Employment has produced a booklet 'Drug Misuse and the Workplace – A Guide for Employers'.

Confederation of British Industry (CBI)
(in association with Turning Point - see **Advice and counselling**)
Centre Point
103 Oxford Street
London WC1A 1DU
The CBI and Turning Point have produced a booklet 'Danger – Drugs at Work'.

Health Education Authority
Hamilton House
Mabledon Place
London WC1H 9TX
Tel: 071 383 3833
For all aspects of health in the workplace.

Health and Safety Executive (HSE)
(See the telephone directory for local office)
The HSE gives advice on health problems which may result from drugs in the workplace. It has produced a booklet 'Drug Abuse at Work – A Guide to Employers'.

THE TREATMENT OF DRUG MISUSE AND DEPENDENCY

TREATMENT PRACTICE

HISTORY

Treatment of addiction has evolved on a formal basis since the first controls over addictive drugs were introduced in the UK in 1920. This legislation preserved the principle that doctors could prescribe controlled drugs to addicts in medical care.

In 1926 the Rolleston Committee reviewed procedures and laid down the foundations for the so-called 'British system' of treatment, formalising when it would be appropriate to prescribe morphine or heroin to addicts. This included addicts under treatment for cure by gradual withdrawal and maintenance cases where, after every effort to cure the addiction, the drug could not be completely withdrawn.

Maintenance doses, often over a long period of time, were allowed when complete withdrawal would produce serious symptoms which could not be satisfactorily treated. They could also be prescribed to patients who, while able to lead a useful and fairly normal life when taking a steady and usually small dose, could not do so once the allowance was withdrawn.

In the early 1960s there was a significant rise in the number of addicts being treated, especially for heroin. The Brain Committee (1965) drew attention to overprescribing by a very small number of doctors as a significant cause. As a result, prescribing of heroin and cocaine was restricted to doctors specially licensed by the Home Office. Since these restrictions were implemented in 1968 by the Dangerous Drugs (Supply to Addicts) Regulations, other drugs, notably dipipanone (Diconal), have been injudiciously prescribed. This drug was similarly restricted in 1984 following a recommendation by the Advisory Council on the Misuse of Drugs in their report 'Treatment and Rehabilitation'.

The report led to the DHSS setting up a working group and 'Guidelines of Good Clinical Practice in the Treatment of Drug Misuse' were formulated and published in 1984. For the first time these flexible guidelines were available to help all doctors – whether they were family doctors, casualty officers, psychiatrists, police surgeons or prison medical officers – when they were confronted by a patient needing treatment for drug misuse.

The term 'treatment' was construed as overall care of the drug user and not just synonymous with prescribing the drug of dependence or a substitute. The importance of support services, friends and family involvement was stressed, together with long-term care and rehabilitation, with the aim of eventually achieving a drug-free lifestyle.

Treatment included prescribing a controlled drug but, if opioids were indicated, doctors were strongly advised to supply only oral preparations such as methadone mixture DTF 1 mg/ml, such preparations being less attractive to the illicit market. Long-term prescribing of opioids was not advised except in consultation with a specialist from a drug treatment clinic or another expert.

A full assessment of the patient was deemed necessary before controlled drugs were prescribed. This included verification of the history of drug-taking with the family, friends, previous doctors and other professionals, and the Addicts' Index to ensure that claims were genuine. The patient then underwent a full physical examination which included urine and blood tests.

Doctors were encouraged to inform the user clearly and sympathetically at their first meeting that treatment would not necessarily include prescribing opioids or barbiturates, and would not involve long-term maintenance. If detoxification were undertaken, an agreement or 'contract' was made between the doctor and the user so that both were aware of what was expected of the other. If it was found that the withdrawal schedule was too demanding on the patient, the 'contract' could be renegotiated. The doctor was warned against being drawn unwittingly into a long-term maintenance programme.

In summary, the Guidelines focused on opiates (these being seen to be the major problems at the time) and achieving withdrawal as soon as possible. New Guidelines are soon to be published; these will take account of the current prevalent misuse of cocaine, amphetamines and other stimulants, and of hallucinogens.

AIDS AND DRUG ABUSE

Treatment philosophy was radically reconsidered following a further report by the Advisory Council on the Misuse of Drugs entitled 'Aids and Drug Misuse Part I', published in 1988. The report highlighted the need to take immediate action to tackle the spread of the Human Immunodeficiency Virus or HIV infection through injecting drug misuse. To avoid a tragedy of enormous proportions, it was recognised that effective preventive action had to be taken to slow down the rate at which the virus was spreading.

The report unequivocally stated that *HIV IS A GREATER THREAT TO PUBLIC AND INDIVIDUAL HEALTH THAN DRUG MISUSE.*

AIDS or Acquired Immune Deficiency Syndrome was first identified in 1981 in the USA. It is a fatal condition that can develop after being infected by the HIV. To date there is no effective treatment that can stop the virus spreading throughout the body and destroying the immune system.

Since the first reported cases, the disease has spread with frightening rapidity. There have been almost 4,800 cases of AIDS reported in the UK, of these 2,747 people (58 per cent) are known to have died. The cumulative total for HIV antibody positive reports for the UK is 15,837 (Department of Health press release 7 August 1991).

HIV infection is transferred through the exchange of certain body fluids such as blood and semen. It has been established that the main means of transfer are:

- Sexual intercourse (both heterosexual and homosexual).
- Using shared and contaminated needles, syringes and other equipment by injecting drug users.
- Using contaminated blood and blood products for medical purposes.
- Infecting unborn babies by their HIV-infected mothers.

Research has indicated that 16 per cent of known cases of HIV infection in the UK were caused by using contaminated drug injecting equipment. This figure varied quite considerably from area to area with rates as high as 50 per cent in parts of Edinburgh to nil in other parts of the UK. If the pattern abroad is followed, infection within the injecting drug-user community will represent a major route by which the virus may spread into the wider community.

In 1987 the UK Government took action against the spread of the virus through injecting drug misuse by:

- A publicity campaign to warn drug users of the dangers of injecting and sharing equipment.
- Providing extra resources to help drug misuse services play a growing role in the fight against AIDS.
- Establishing 15 pilot schemes where users could exchange used needles and syringes for new.

In 1988 the Advisory Council on the Misuse of Drugs presented their report on Aids and Drug Misuse and the present treatment model and practice to combat HIV and drugs misuse evolved.

CURRENT PRACTICE

Attention is now directed at a far wider section of drug misusers. Drug services must target all those whose actions involve, or may lead to, the sharing of injecting equipment.

Drug misusers are encouraged to enter a treatment regime and are informed of the dangers of HIV infection and how to avoid or reduce risks by *not sharing syringes and needles* and *not having unprotected sexual intercourse.*

In support, a network of centres is being established which provide free condoms and exchange needles and syringes; pharmacists are encouraged to sell needles and syringes; advice is readily available regarding the cleaning of injecting equipment; and a local and national education and information system is being established.

There has been an increase in treatment services in virtually every part of the country through specialist centres attached to hospitals or community drug services working with local doctors. It is Government policy to encourage GPs to treat drug misusers, including addicts.

The ultimate objective is to withdraw the individual from drugs completely. However, the way of achieving this goal is far more flexible than in the past. If a user is not ready to move directly towards abstinence a full range of treatment options, including longer-term prescribing, is available. It is imperative that treatment is tailored to an individual's needs to ensure that he remains in contact.

A flexible prescribing practice plays an important part in assisting the user to achieve intermediate goals such as:

- The cessation of sharing injecting equipment;
- Moving from injectable to oral drug use;
- Decreasing drug use; and finally
- Abstinence.

Drug users may seek medical help from either a specialist unit at a hospital or from a local doctor. A medical examination takes place together with a full assessment to establish the user's needs. The GP may refer the individual to the specialist hospital unit for the assessment. In either case the hospital may refer the person back to his GP to continue treatment.

Although a doctor can still prescribe heroin, cocaine and dipipanone to relieve pain from organic disease or injury, he can only prescribe those drugs for the purposes of addiction if licensed by the Home Office. Licensed doctors are mainly attached to the Drug Dependency Units in hospitals.

When a user consults a doctor as a private patient, the doctor is allowed to charge an unrestricted fee for consultation. If necessary, the doctor will issue the patient with a private prescription which is dispensed at a pharmacy, and the pharmacist will charge a fee which includes the cost of the drug itself. It should be born in mind that some drugs are very expensive and a week's supply could cost in excess of £100.

The Misuse of Drugs (Notification of and Supply to Addicts) Regulations 1973 require any doctor attending a person considered to be addicted to certain controlled drugs to notify the Chief Medical Officer at the Home Office. Additional information in respect of whether drugs are injected is now also requested.

This forms the basis of the Addicts' Index which is used for statistical analysis, as a check against addicts seeking treatment from more than one source, and as a means of monitoring prescribing.

LOCAL DRUGS SERVICE

The following pages (180–186) list hospital and health centre services that provide treatment for people with drug problems. Many can admit patients to hospital to detoxify or stabilise them and all will see drug users as out-patients. Most will allow drug users to refer themselves for treatment, many will first want a telephone call to arrange an appointment and some will require the referral to be made by a GP.

Many specialist drug services are community based, usually in the centre of towns or close to main shopping centres. A selection of these has been listed (pages 187–193). They provide a wide range of services, including counselling, advice and information. Usually they work closely with the specialist hospital service for the area or with local doctors. Some have a doctor on their staff.

For people who wish to learn to live without drugs but cannot do so without moving away from where they are living, there are residential rehabilitation centres throughout the country. Drug users may live at a centre from a few months to over a year. How long they stay will depend on the problems a drug user has and the help needed to overcome these. A selection of these centres is listed on pages 194–201.

There are a number of private treatment centres and nursing homes which also offer treatment and care for people with drug and alcohol problems. There is a charge for these, often paid for by medical insurance or by the individual or the family. These have not been listed but details of them can be obtained from SCODA (see below).

The Standing Conference on Drug Abuse (SCODA)
1–4 Hatton Place
Hatton Garden
London EC1N 8ND
Tel: 071 430 2341

NHS HOSPITAL AND HEALTH CENTRE SERVICES

The following services are managed by local Health Authorities. Many are sited in hospitals or hospital grounds, although increasingly they are now found in buildings in the community.

The services which they offer will vary from area to area. The majority have a doctor in charge, can provide out-patient and in-patient help and will prescribe substitute drugs to help the drug user gradually become drug-free.

Most will only take patients from their own catchment area, usually the Health Authority. They can be extremely busy and may at times have a waiting list.

Some services will only accept referrals made by a family doctor or by another professional person, such as a specialist drug worker, a probation officer or a social worker. Some may require an appointment to be made. The majority of these services now accept self-referrals, but where there are exceptions, this is shown.

England is divided into 14 Regional Health Authorities (RHAs) and the hospital and health centre services have been listed by the RHA in which they are based. The services in Northern Ireland and Wales have been listed alphabetically by their location and in Scotland they have been listed by north, south, east and west Scotland.

SOUTH WEST THAMES RHA

Regional Drug Dependency Unit
Department of Addictive Behaviour
Clare House
St George's Hospital
Blackshaw Road
London SW17
Tel: 081 672 9881
In- and out-patient

Addiction Treatment Centre
Queen Mary's University Hospital
Roehampton Lane
London SW15 5PN
Tel: 081 789 6611 ext 2309
In- and out-patient

Queen's Road Day Hospital
Drug Dependency Clinic
Queen's Road
Croydon CR9 2PQ
Tel: 081 684 8458
In and out-patient

Community Drug and Alcohol Team
Department of Psychiatry
Epsom General Hospital
Dorking Road
Epsom
Surrey KT18 7EG
Tel: 0372 726100 ext 6363
Out-patient

Drug Dependency Clinic
Brookwood Hospital
Knaphill
Woking
Surrey GU21 2RQ
Tel: 0483 474545
In- and out-patient by GP referral

Crawley Hospital
Substance Abuse Project
West Green Drive
Crawley RH11 7DH
Tel: 0293 551134
In- and out-patient

The Summit Substance Misuse Team
22 Sutley Road
Bognor Regis
West Sussex PO21 1ER
Tel. 0243 869234
In- and out-patient

SOUTH EAST THAMES RHA

Substance Misuse Unit
South Western Hospital
Landor House
Landor Road
Stockwell
London SW9
Tel: 071 326 5450
In- and out-patient

The Blackfriars Road Drug Dependency Unit
St George's Clinic
151 Blackfriars Road
London SE1 8EL
Tel: 071 620 0192
Out-patient

Drug Dependence Out-Patient Department
The Maudsley Hospital
Denmark Hill
London SE5 8AZ
Tel: 071 703 6333 ext 2340
In- and out-patient

Brighton Drug Dependency Service
Herbert Hone Clinic
11 Buckingham Road
Brighton BN1 3RA
Tel: 0273 23395
In- and out-patient (for opiate users only)

Drug Dependency Unit
St Helen's Hospital
Frederick Road
Hastings
East Sussex TN34 5AH
Tel: 0424 720088
In- and out-patient

NORTH WEST THAMES RHA

Brent Community Drug Service
Central Middlesex Hospital
194 Kilburn High Road
London NW6
Tel: 071 624 2001/2077
Out-patient by appointment

St Mary's Hospital
Drug Dependency Centre
16 South Wharf Road
Praed Street
London W2
Tel: 071 725 6666
Out-patient

Charing Cross Hospital
Drug Dependency Unit
9 Wolverton Gardens
London W6 7DQ
Tel: 081 846 7766
Out-patient

Gate House Clinic
St Bernard's Wing
Ealing Hospital
Uxbridge Road
Southall
Middlesex UB1 3EU
Tel: 081 574 2444 ext 5192
Limited in-patient and out-patient by appointment

West Middlesex Hospital
Drug Dependency Clinic
Twickenham Road
Isleworth TW7 6AF
Tel: 081 565 5071
Out-patient by appointment

St Mary Abbotts' Drug Dependency Unit
Marloes Road
Kensington
London W8 5LQ
Tel: 081 846 6111
Out-patient

Community Alcohol and Drug Service
Queen Elizabeth II Hospital
Howlands
Welwyn Garden City
AL7 4HQ
Hertfordshire
Tel: 0707 328111 ext 4636
In- and out-patient

North Herts Substance Misuse Team
Department of Psychiatry
Lister Hospital
Coreys Mill Lane
Stevenage
Hertfordshire
Tel: 0438 314333
In- and out-patient

NORTH EAST THAMES RHA

Drug Dependency Unit
The London Hospital
(St Clements)
2a Bow Road
London E3 4LL
Tel: 081 377 7975
Out-patient by appointment

Drug Dependency Clinic
University College Hospital
122 Hampstead Road
London NW1 2LT
Tel: 071 387 9541
Out-patient

Drug Dependency Clinic
Hackney Hospital
Homerton High Street
London E9 6BE
Tel: 081 986 6816
Out-patient

Southend Drug Advisory and Treatment Service
The Roche Unit
c/o District Office
Union Lane
Rochford
Essex SS4 1RB
Tel: 0702 541516
In- and out-patient

WESSEX RHA

Drugs Advice Centre
Northern Road
Cosham
Portsmouth PO6 3EP
Tel: 0705 324636
Professional advice, information, counselling, onward referral and short-term treatment unit.
In and out-patient

Department of Psychiatry
Royal South Hants Hospital
Graham Road
Southampton S09 4PE
Tel: 0703 634288
In- and out-patient

OXFORD RHA

Regional Drug Problem Team
Chilton Clinic
Warneford Hospital
Warneford Lane
Headington
Oxford OX3 7JX
Tel: 0865 226243
In- and out-patient

SOUTH WESTERN RHA

Avon Drug Problem Team
Glenside Hospital
Blackberry Hill
Bristol BS16 1DD
Tel: 0272 584444
In- and out-patient by appointment only

District Addictions Service
39 Abbey Road
Torquay
Devon TQ2 5NQ
Tel: 0803 291129
Out patient

EAST ANGLIA RHA

Drug Dependency Unit
The Mill House
Brookfields Hospital
351 Mill Road
Cambridge CB1 3DF
Tel: 0223 245926
In- and out-patient

The Bure Clinic
West Norwich Hospital
Bowthorpe Road
Norwich NR2 3TU
Tel: 0603 667955
In and out-patient

WEST MIDLANDS RHA

Drug Addiction Unit
All Saints Hospital
Lodge Road
Birmingham B18 5SD
Tel: 021 523 5151
In- and out-patient by professional referral

TRENT RHA

John Storer Clinic
Amberley Street
Nottingham NG1 6HD
Tel: 0602 418964
In- and out-patient

Drug Dependency Unit
Royal Hallamshire Hospital
Glossop Road
Sheffield S10 2JF
Tel: 0742 766222
In- and out-patient

NORTH WESTERN RHA

Regional Drug Dependence Unit
Prestwich Hospital
Bury New Road
Prestwich
Manchester M25 7BL
Tel: 061 773 9121 ext 3118
In- and out-patient (referral from and to Community Drug Teams)

Rochdale Community Drug Team
162a Birch Road
Town Hall Square
Rochdale
Lancashire OL16 1NJ
Tel: 0706 861515
Referral to Prestwich Hospital

YORKSHIRE RHA

District Addictions Service
The Portakabin
St Mary's Hospital
Dean Road
Scarborough
North Yorkshire YO12 7SN
Tel: 0723 371691
Out-patient

Community Addictions Team
c/o Knaresborough Hospital
Stockwell Lane
Knaresborough
North Yorkshire HG5 0JG
Tel: 0423 868549
In- and out-patient

Sumit
Sumit Lodge
2 Slutwell Lane
Pontefract
West Yorkshire WF8 1EA
Tel: 0977 606888
In- and out-patient

Leeds Addiction Unit
19 Springfield Mount
Leeds LS2 9LF
Tel: 0532 423182
Out-patient and day centre

MERSEY RHA

Warrington Drug Dependency Clinic
9 Wilson Patten Street
Warrington WA1 1PG
Tel: 0925 415176
In- and out-patient

Widnes and Halton Drug Dependency Unit
The Rear
39–41 Victoria Road
Widnes
Tel: 051 423 5247
In- and out-patient

Merseyside Regional Drug Dependency Clinic
Countess of Chester Hospital
Liverpool Road
Chester CH2 1BQ
Tel: 0244 364100
Act as referral to relevant clinic for patients
outside catchment.
In- and out-patient

Liverpool Drug Dependency Clinic
10 Maryland Street
Liverpool
Tel: 051 709 0516
In- and out-patient by professional referral

Southport Drug Dependency Clinic
46 Houghton Street
Southport
Tel: 0704 533133 ext 2525
Out-patient

Wirral Drug Service
New Lodge
St Catherine's Hospital
Tranmere
Birkenhead
Tel: 051 652 0002
In- and out-patient by appointment only

NORTHERN RHA

Regional Alcohol and Drug Problem Service
Plummer Court
Carliol Place
Newcastle-upon-Tyne NE1 6UR
Tel: 091 230 1300
In- and out-patient

WALES

Gwynedd Drugs Advisory Service
11a Vaughan Street
Llandudno
Gwynedd
Tel: 0492 875427
In- and out-patient

Drug Addiction Treatment Unit
Whitchurch Hospital
Park Road
Whitchurch
Cardiff CF4 7XB
Tel: 0222 693191
In- and out patient

Gwent Drug Clinic
Bettws Ward
c/o St Cadoc's Hospital
Caerleon
Gwent
Tel: 0633 421121 ext 211
In- and out-patient

Powys Drugs and Alcohol Council
Problem Substance Abuse Department
Mid Wales Hospital
Talgarth
Powys LD3 0S
Tel: 0874 711073
In- and out-patient

SCOTLAND

North

Dunain House Addiction Unit
Craig Dunain Hospital
Inverness IV3 6JU
Tel: 0463 234101
In- and out-patient by professional or self-referral

Royal Cornhill Hospital
Cornhill Road
Aberdeen AB9 2ZH
Tel: 0224 681818 ext 57529
In- and out-patient; GP referral preferred

Bilbohall Hospital
34 Pluscarden Road
Elgin
Tel: 0343 3131 ext 256
Out-patient; GP referral preferred

South

Dingleton Hospital
Melrose TD9 9HN
Tel: 0896 822727
GP referral

Heston House
Crichton Royal Hospital
Dumfries DG1 4TG
Tel: 0387 55301 ext 2181
In- and out-patient

East

Stratheden Hospital
Springfield
Cupar KY15 5RR
Tel: 0334 52611
In-patient only by GP referral

Community Drug Problem Service
Royal Edinburgh Hospital
Morningside Terrace
Edinburgh EH10 5HF
Tel: 031 447 2011
In- and out-patient

Royal Dundee Liff Hospital
Dundee DD2 5NF
Tel: 0382 580441
Referral via Drug Problem Centre

Psychiatric Division
Bellsdyke Hospital
Larbert
Tel: 0324 556131
GP referral

West

Drug Abuse Team
Monklands District General Hospital
Monkscourt Avenue
Airdrie ML6
Tel: 02364 69344 ext 305
GP referral preferred

Ailsa Hospital
Dalmellington Road
Ayr KA6 6AB
Tel: 0292 65136
In- and out-patient

Alcohol and Drug Problems Unit
Hartwood Hospital
Hartwood
Shotts ML7 4LA
Tel: 0501 23366 ext 338
GP referral preferred

Drug Group
Southern General Hospital
1345 Govan Road
Glasgow G51 4TF
Tel: 041 440 0741
In- and out-patient

Community Alcohol Service
Leverndale Hospital
26 Florence Street
Glasgow G5
Tel: 041 429 8292
Out-patient

Duke Street Hospital
Carswell House
5 Oakley Terrace
Glasgow G31 2HX
Tel: 041 554 6267
Out-patient by GP referral only

NORTHERN IRELAND

Northern Ireland Regional Unit
Shaftesbury Square Hospital
116–122 Great Victoria Street
Belfast BT2 7BG
Tel: 0232 329808
Information on facilities throughout Northern Ireland

ADVISORY AND COUNSELLING SERVICES

Advisory and counselling services are community based and provide a wide range of services. These may include information, primary health care, advice, counselling, group work, substitute prescribing, needle and syringe exchange, home visits, detached work and referral to other specialist services such as in-patient units and residential rehabilitation.

The services may be managed by Health Authorities or by voluntary organisations. All have paid staff and some additionally use volunteers.

The following list is not exhaustive, but is representative of the organisations that exist to help drug users throughout the United Kingdom. At the time of publication the list is up to date. If there is any difficulty contacting an organisation, or if there is not one listed for your area, SCODA may be able to give you a more local contact (see page 168).

The services have been listed by geographical region for England and alphabetically by location for Scotland and Wales. For Northern Ireland, see the Northern Ireland Regional Unit on page 186.

LONDON

Blenheim Project
7 Thorpe Close
London W10 5XL
Tel: 081 960 5599

Community Drug Project (CDP)
30 Manor Place
London SE17 3BB
Tel: 071 703 0559

Hungerford Drug Project
32a Wardour Street
London W1V 3HJ
Tel: 071 437 3523

Kaleidoscope Youth and Community Project
40–46 Cromwell Road
Kingston-upon-Thames
Surrey KT2 6RE
Tel: 081 549 2681/7488

Hackney Community Drug Team
62 Kenworthy Road
Hackney
London E9 5RA
Tel: 081 986 0660

Drug Advisory Service Haringey (DASH)
St Ann's Centre for Health Care
St Ann's Road
London N15 3TH
Tel: 081 802 0443

The Angel Project
38–44 Liverpool Road
London N1 0PU
Tel: 071 354 4777

The Newham Drug Project
39 Wellington Road
London E6 2RQ
Tel: 081 552 7225

East London Drug Project
Oxford House
Derbyshire Street
Bethnal Green
London E2 6HE
Tel: 071 729 8008

Drug Concern (Harrow)
44 Bessborough Road
Harrow
Middlesex HA1 3DJ
Tel: 081 864 9622

Drug Concern (Barnet)
Woodlands
Colindale Hospital Grounds
Colindale Avenue
London NW9 5HG
Tel: 081 200 9525/9575

Community Drug Team
Fountains Mill
81 High Street
Uxbridge UB8 1JR
Tel: 0895 250414/5

The Stockwell Project
1/3 Stockwell Gardens
London SW9 0RX
Tel: 071 274 7013

Community Drug Team
11 Windsor Walk
London SE5 8BB
Tel: 071 708 5888

THE SOUTH EAST

Community Substance Abuse Services
Frith Cottage
Church Road
Frimley
Surrey GU16 5AD
Tel: 0276 62566

West Suffolk Drug Advisory Service
18 St John Street
Bury St Edmunds
Suffolk IP33 1SJ
Tel: 0284 762377

NW Surrey Substance Misuse Team
Abraham Cowley Unit
Homewood NHS Trust
Holloway Hill
Lyne
Chertsey
Tel: 0932 872010 ext 3309

DAIS (Drug Advice and Information Service)
38 West Street
Brighton BN1 2RE
Tel: 0273 21000

Healthlink
Drugs and Alcohol Advisory Service
55 St Peter's Street
Bedford MK40 2PR
Tel: 0234 270123

The Drug Unit and Neutral Zone
156 Oxford Road
Reading RG1 7PJ
Tel: 0734 391452

Bucks Council on Alcohol and Drugs
Tindal Cottage
Bierton Road
Aylesbury
Buckinghamshire HP20 1EN
Tel: 0296 25329

Milestones
East Lodge
Bexley Hospital
1 Old Bexley Lane
Bexley
Kent DA5 2BW
Tel: 0322 5559058

Peterborough Community Drug Team
City Health Clinic
Wellington Street
Peterborough
Cambridgeshire
Tel: 0733 898383

Druglink
Trefoil House
Red Lion Lane
Hemel Hempstead
Hertfordshire HP3 9TE
Tel: 0923 260733

Stevenage Drugsline
Volunteer Centre
Swingate
Stevenage SG1 1RU
Tel: 0438 364067

Addiction Centre
4 Manor Road
Chatham
Kent ME4 6AG
Tel: 0634 830114

Oxford District Drug and Alcohol Community Team
The Ley Clinic
Littlemore Hospital
Oxford OX4 4XN
Tel: 0865 223276

Bridge Project
154 Mill Road
Cambridge CB1 3LP
Tel: 0223 214614

THE SOUTH WEST

BADAS (Bath Area Drugs Advisory Service)
1–2 Bridewell Lane
Bath
Tel: 0225 469479

Bristol Drugs Project
18 Guinea Street
Redcliffe
Bristol BS1 6SX
Tel: 0272 298047

Freshfield Service
1st Floor
10 Strangeways Terrace
Truro TR1 2NY
Tel: 0872 41952

Exeter Drugs Project
59 Magdalen Street
Exeter EX2 4HY
Tel: 0392 410292

Plymouth Community Drug Service
Nuffield Clinic
Seventrees
Lipson Road
Plymouth PL4 8NQ
Tel: 0752 660281

East Dorset Community Drugs Team
Park Lodge
Royal Victoria Hospital
Gloucester Road
Boscombe
Bournemouth BH7 8NQ
Tel: 0202 397003

Gloucestershire Drug Project
24 Cambray Place
Cheltenham GL50 1JN
Tel: 0242 570003

Portsmouth Drug Advice Centre
Northern Road Clinic
Northern Road
Cosham
Portsmouth PO6 3EP
Tel: 0705 324636

Median: Winchester Drug Advisory Service
St Paul's Hospital
St Paul's Hill
Winchester SO22 5AA
Tel: 0962 840900

Druglink
Drug Advisory Centre
174 Victoria Road
Swindon
Wiltshire
Tel: 0793 610133

Salisbury Alcohol and Drug Advisory Service
1 The Paragon
Wilton Road
Salisbury
Wiltshire SP2 7EH
Tel: 0722 412632

THE MIDLANDS

Community Drug Service
27a St Owen Street
Hereford HR1 2JB
Tel: 0432 263636

Derby Drugline
2nd Floor
Willow House
Willow Row
Derby DE1 2NZ
Tel: 0332 382954

Substance Misuse Service
Newton Hospital
Newton Road
Worcester WR5 1JG
Tel: 0905 763333 ext 33249

Community Drug Service
Paget House
2 West Street
Leicester LE1 6XP
Tel: 0533 470200

Alcohol and Drug Counselling Service
Portland House
3 Portland Street
Lincoln
Tel: 0522 521908

Coventry Community Drug Team
2 Dover Street
Coventry CV1 3DD
Tel: 0203 553845

South Birmingham Community Drug Team
The Mary Street Centre
213 Mary Street
Balsall Heath B12 9RN
Tel: 021 440 4444

North Staffs Community Drug Team
76–82 Hope Street
Hanley
Stoke-on-Trent ST1 5BX
Tel: 0782 202139

Drugline
Dale House
New Meeting Street
Birmingham B4 7SX
Tel: 021 632 6363

Advice on Addiction
Stafford Drugline
92 Wolverhampton Road
Stafford ST17 4AH
Tel: 0785 51820

THE NORTH EAST

Community Drugs and Alcohol Advice Service
29 Yarm Lane
Stockton-on-Tees
Cleveland TS18 3DT
Tel: 0642 607313

DATA (Drug Advice Treatment Agency)
30A Doncaster Road
Scunthorpe
Tel: 0724 856948

Drug Advisory Service and Helpline
63 King's Road
North Ormesby
Middlesbrough
Cleveland TS3 6EP
Tel: 0642 242550

Alcohol and Drug Advisory Centre
10 Grange Road
Hartlepool TS26 8JA
Tel: 0429 863046

Hull and East Yorkshire Council for Drug Problems
6 Wright Street
Hull HU2 8HU
Tel: 0482 225868

North East Council on Addictions
1 Mosely Street
Newcastle-upon-Tyne NE1 1YE
Tel: 091 232 0797

Street Level
The Vicarage
Stanhope Parade
South Shields NE33 4BA
Tel: 091 455 3027

Sunderland District Community Addictions Team (CAT)
11 Norfolk Street
Sunderland
Tel: 091 510 8933

North Tyneside Alcohol and Drug Problem Service
1 Cleveland Road
North Shields NE29 0NG
Tel: 091 258 7047

York Drugs Resource Scheme
74 Skeldergate
York Y01 1DN
Tel: 0904 647474

Rotherham Community Drugs Team
Medway House
3 Chatham Street
Rotherham
Tel: 0709 382733

Rockingham Drug Project
117 Rockingham Street
Sheffield S1 4EB
Tel: 0742 580033 (Helpline)

The Bridge Project
Equity Chambers
40 Piccadilly
Bradford BD1 3NN
Tel: 0274 723863

THE NORTH WEST

Lifeline Warrington
45 Wilson Patten Street
Warrington WA1
Tel: 0925 53261

Dependency Service
Croft House
Wigton Road
Carlisle CA1 3FP
Tel: 0228 49605

South Cumbria Community Drug Team
Prospect House
3 Prospect Road
Barrow-in-Furness
Tel: 0229 833004

Merseyside Drugs Council
27 Hope Street
Liverpool L1 9BQ
Tel: 051 709 0074

Blackpool CDT
Whitegate Health Centre
156 Whitegate Drive
Blackpool FY3 9HG
Tel: 0253 63232

Manchester Drug Advice Centre
101–103 Oldham Street
Manchester M4 1LW
Tel: 061 839 2054

Lancaster Community Drug Team
Ryelands House Clinic
Ryelands Park
Lancaster LA1 2LN
Tel: 0524 66354

Mersey Regional Drug Training and Information Centre
27 Hope Street
Liverpool L1 9BQ
Tel: 051 709 3511

Community Drug Team
Workington Infirmary
Infirmary Road
Workington
Cumbria CA14 2UN
Tel: 0900 68739

WALES

Clwyd Drugs Prevention Service
21b Chester Road West
Shotton
Tel: 0244 831798

Camarthen Drugs Project
The Lodge
1 Penlan Road
Carmarthen
Dyfed SA31 1DN
Tel: 0267 222107

South Gwent Drug Project
139 Lower Dock Street
Newport NP9 1EE
Tel: 0633 216777

Pembrokeshire Drugs Team
Priory Street
Milford Haven
Pembrokeshire
Tel: 0646 690327

Llanelli Drugs Project
4a Cowell Street
Llanelli SA15 1UU
Tel: 0554 756273

Mid Glamorgan CDT
Llwyn-yr-eos Clinic
Main Road
Church Village
Pontypridd
Mid Glamorgan C538 1RN
Tel: 0443 217026

Community Drugs Team
46 Cowbridge Road East
Canton
Cardiff CF1 9DU
Tel: 0222 395877/8

Swansea Drugs Project (SAND)
8 Calvert Terrace
Swansea SA1 6AR
Tel: 0792 472002

SCOTLAND

Leith Community Drug Project
3 Smiths Place
Leith
Edinburgh
Tel: 031 554 7516

Falkirk District Drugs Project
3–5 Chapel Lane
Falkirk FK1 5BB
Tel: 0324 612627

Aberdeen Drugs Action
8A Gaelic Lane
Aberdeen
Tel: 0224 624555

Drug and Alcohol Project
99 Rowan Street
Blackburn
Bathgate EH47 7ED
Tel: 0506 634898

Muirhouse/Pilton Drug Project
Department of Social Work
34 Muirhouse Crescent
Edinburgh EH4 4QL
Tel: 031 343 1991

Castle Project
PO Box 922
Edinburgh EH16 1DU
Tel: 031 652 1605

SHADA
Unit 15
Muirhouse Shopping Centre
10 Pennywell Court
Edinburgh EH14 4TZ
Tel: 031 332 2314

Simpson House Drug Project
52 Queen Street
Edinburgh EH2 3NS
Tel: 031 225 1054

WEST
8/4 Murrayburn Park
Wester Hailes
Edinburgh
Tel: 031 442 2465

Bridge Project
17 River Street
Ayr
Tel: 0292 287777

Kilmarnock Drugs Project
Portacabin
Bentinck Centre
East Netherton Street
Kilmarnock KA1 4AX
Tel: 0563 43700

Townhead Addiction Centre
45 Townhead
Irvine KA12 0BH
Tel: 0294 75631

ECODA
8/12 Arnisdale Road
Easterhouse
Glasgow G34 9BU
Tel: 041 773 2001

G21 Drug Group
The Basement
311 Roystonhill
Glasgow G21 2HN
Tel: 041 552 5361

Possil Drug Project
101 Denmark Street
Possil Park
Glasgow G22 5AU
Tel: 041 336 3365

Inverclyde Drugline
3 Shaw Place
Greenock
Tel: 0475 888053

Addiction Information Centre
234 Kinfauns Drive
Drumchapel
Glasgow G15 7AH
Tel: 041 944 4242

Cambuslang Addiction Project
13 Main Street
Cambuslang G72 7EX
Tel: 041 641 7038

Castlemilk Drug Project
9/11 Ballantay Quadrant
Castlemilk
Glasgow G45 0DY
Tel: 041 634 0711

East End Drugs Initiative
170 Stamford Street
Barrowfield
Glasgow G31 4AP
Tel: 041 556 7200

Addiction Advisory Centre
81c Hallcraig Street
Airdrie ML6 6AN
Tel: 0236 53263

Candle Addiction Advice Centre
5 South Muirhead Road
Cumbernauld G67 1AX
Tel: 0236 735539

Drug Problem Centre
Dudhope House
15 Dudhope Terrace
Dundee
Tel: 0382 25083

RESIDENTIAL REHABILITATION AND TREATMENT SERVICES

This list covers residential projects for drug users. They are generally designed for people who wish to stop using drugs and to learn to live without drugs. Some of the services are able to offer detoxification and rehabilitation, but the majority require the drug user to be drug-free for at least 24 hours before admission.

There are a small number of very specialised services, for instance for drug users in drug crisis or drug users with AIDS. These have not been listed but information about these services can be obtained from SCODA (see page 168) and some new services will open shortly.

Residential rehabilitation and treatment services vary from one service to another, not only in respect of the age and sex of the person who can be accepted, but also on how long the person is expected to stay, what kind of rehabilitation programme is offered, etc. If a court has imposed a 'condition of residence' order (i.e. a condition requiring a defendant to reside at a particular address or particular type of residence) on a drug user, it is indicated whether or not a residence will accept that person.

Broadly, the services may be divided into **general houses** which provide accommodation, support and individual and group counselling; and **therapeutic communities** with a more hierarchical structure. In therapeutic communities, residents work their way up the hierarchy, accepting more responsibility for themselves and the running of the house as they progress through the programme. In some houses, the Christian belief of the resident is an important factor and in some others the houses are run by Christian staff. Brief information about the main conditions and types of residence are given below.

Finally, it should be noted that most residential services will accept people from anywhere in the country. It is often felt better that a drug user goes to a different area to learn how to become drug-free to avoid previous associations with drug use.

LONDON

Alwin House
40 Colville Terrace
London W11
Tel: 071 229 0311

Mixed
Age: 18–25
Bed spaces: 6

Residential support group plus full-time staff. Voluntary referrals only. Drug-free on entry. Cannot accommodate children but will take couples.

Crescent House (Richmond Fellowship)
10 St Stephen's Crescent
London W2
Tel: 071 229 3710

Mixed
Age: 17+
Bed spaces: 14

Group or individual counselling. Drug-free for 24 hours before admission. Cannot accommodate children or couples. Will *not* accept people with a 'condition of residence' order.

Elizabeth House
94 Redcliffe Gardens
London SW10 9HH
Tel: 071 370 1279

Mixed
Age: 26–38
Bed spaces: 7

Resident support group plus full-time staff. Voluntary referrals only. Drug-free on entry. Cannot accommodate children but will take couples.

The Maya Project
14–16 Peckham Hill Street
London SE15 6BN
Tel: 071 635 5070

Women only
Age: Any
Bed spaces: 8 adults, 4 children (any age)

Priority given to women from the black communities. Pregnant women will be accepted. The programme is structured around the needs of each individual. Referrals from any source. Drug-free on admission. Cannot accommodate couples.

Number 30 (Richmond Fellowship)
30 St Charles' Square
London W10 6EE
Tel: 081 969 0503

Women only
Age: 18+
Bed spaces: 6 single parents, 8 children 0–11 years

A non-medical opiate detoxification programme (10 days) and recovery programme (eight weeks). Group work, individual work and child work. Separate aftercare facility for those who have completed the programme. Do *not* accept people on 'condition of residence' order.

Oak Lodge
136 West Hill
London SW15
Tel: 081 788 1648

Mixed
Age: 17+
Bed spaces: 14

Democratic structure. Drug-free on admission. Self-referral. Group sessions are compulsory.

Phoenix House
1 Eliot Bank
London SE23
Tel: 081 699 5748/1515

Mixed
Age: 16+
Bed spaces: 81 (4 sites)

Drug-free 24 hours before admission. Can accommodate children and will take couples. Will take people with 'condition of residence' order.

Two-Three-Five Project
235 Balham High Road
London SW17
Tel: 081 672 9464

Mixed
Age: 18+
Bed spaces: 12

Hostel for ex-offenders and ex-drug or alcohol addicts. A minimum support unit that can be used as a stepping stone to independent living. Referrals should be drug-free.

THE SOUTH EAST

Cranstoun Project
5 Ember Lane
Esher
Surrey
Tel: 081 398 6956

Mixed
Age: 17+
Bed spaces: 10

Self-catering democratic community. Group or individual counselling. Drug-free on entry. Cannot accommodate children or couples. Will accept people on 'condition of residence' orders.

The Hove Family Project
Phoenix House
19 Seafield Road
Hove
East Sussex BN3 2TP
Admissions: 071 407 2789
Tel: 0273 220010

Mixed
Age: 16+
Bed spaces: 8 adults, 4 children under 12

Three to six months family programme designed to maintain each family's independence. Programme devised around the needs of the individual. All applicants must be either former drug users or receiving methadone on prescription from a doctor. Pregnant women will be considered for admission as will parents who use illicit drugs but who wish to become stable. Will accept people with 'condition of residence' order.

Pheonix House
Colwell Court
1 Pages Avenue
Bexhill on Sea
East Sussex
Tel: 0424 732171

Mixed
Age: 18+
Bed spaces: 28

Therapeutic community. Length of stay approximately 18 months – priority given to referrals from South East Thames.

Yeldall Manor
Blakes Lane
Hare Hatch
Reading RG10 9XR
Tel: 0734 404411

Men only
Age: 20–40
Bed spaces: 20

Drug-free on admission or non-medical withdrawal immediately on admission. Cannot accommodate children or couples. Will take people with 'condition of residence' order. Christian staff.

THE SOUTH WEST

Accommodation for Recovery from Addiction (ARA)
8a Cotham Hill
Bristol BS6 6LF
Tel: 0272 237154

Mixed
Age: 18+
Bed spaces: 16 (+ 5 for women only)

Accommodation project offering housing, counselling and work integration for ex-users. Two mixed houses and one for women only. Residents should be six weeks abstinent prior to entry.

Alpha House
Wickham Road
Droxford
Southampton SO3 1PD
Tel: 0489 8772210

Mixed
Age: 16–40
Bed spaces: 51

Residential therapeutic community. Drug-free 24 hours before admission.

Broadway Lodge
Old Mixon Road
Weston-super-Mare BS24 9NN
Tel: 0934 812319

Mixed
Age: 18+
Bed spaces: 55

A six to eight week programme based on the principles and steps of Alcoholics and Narcotics Anonymous. Accepts medical insurance payments, direct payments from individuals or contributions to the cost of treatment, as well as residents in receipt of income support. Extended care also available at Broadway Lodge.

Coke Hole Trust
70 Junction Road
Andover
Hampshire
Tel: 0264 61745 (Head Office)

Men and women in separate houses
Age: 20–39
Bed spaces: 8–9 men, 8–9 women, 8 children under 12

Drug-free on entry. Cannot accommodate couples but will take children. Do *not* take people with 'condition of residence' order but do take probation service and prison referrals. Christian staff.

Face to Face
Shirley Holms Manor
Shirley Holms
Lymington
Hampshire SO41 8NH
Tel: 0590 683454

Mixed
Aged: 16–55
Bed spaces: 20

Will accept couples. Stay three to six months which is flexible.

The Life Anew Trust
(Clouds House)
East Knoyle
Salisbury
Wiltshire SP3 6BE
Tel: 0747 830733

Mixed
Age: 18+
Bed spaces: 55

A six to eight week programme based on the principles and steps of Alcoholics and Narcotics Anonymous. Accepts medical insurance payments, direct payments from individuals or contributions to the cost of treatment, as well as residents in receipt of income support.

Meta House
133 Princes Road
Westbourne
Bournemouth BH4 9HG
Tel: 0202 764581

Women only
Age: 16–40
Bed spaces: 20

Drug-free 24 hours before admission. Minimum eight months programme. Accepts people on 'condition of residence' order. Cannot accommodate children. Christian staff.

Meta House (The Hannah Project)
129–131 Princess Road
Westbourne
Dorset BH4 9HG
Tel: 0202 764581

Women only
Age: 16–40
Bed spaces: 8 women, 8 children

Drug-free 24 hours before admission. Minimum eight months programme. Accepts people on 'condition of residence' order. Can accommodate children but not couples. Christian staff.

THE MIDLANDS

Ferry Cross Resource Centre
22–24 Colegate
Norwich
Norfolk NR3 1BQ
Tel: 0603 619397/760396 Answerphone
Men only
Age: 16+
Bed spaces: 25

Long-term accommodation for drug users. Drug-free on entry. Individual and group therapy. Will accept people with 'condition of residence' order.

Life for the World Trust
Hebron House
12 Stanley Avenue
Thorpe
Norwich
Tel: 0603 39905

Women only
Age: 18–30
Bed spaces: 5–6

Extended family home. Can accommodate children. Christian staff. Will take people with 'condition of residence' order. Will take people with a psychiatric history. Will take young women who have an alcohol problem only. Children need social services funding.

Ley Community
Sandy Croft
Sandy Lane
Yarnton
Oxford
Tel: 0865 71777 – general enquiries
     08675 3108 – referrals

Mixed
Age: 18–35
Bed spaces: 42

Therapeutic community. Professional and self-referral.

The Mount (Adullam Homes)
31 Milners Lane
Lawley Bank
Telford
Shropshire TF4 2JJ
Tel: 0952 502787

Mixed
Age: 18–35
Bed spaces: 12

Extended family home. Drug-free for 48 hours
on entry. Will sometimes consider
accommodating couples and children. Will
accept people with 'condition of residence'
order. Christian staff.

Willowdene Farm Rehabilitation Centre
Chorley
Near Bridgenorth
Shropshire WV16 6PP
Tel 074632 658

Mixed
Age: 20–40
Bed spaces: 8

Christian staff. Minimum 10 month
programme catering to individual needs.

THE NORTH EAST

Bridge House
Victoria Villas
311 Allerton Road
Bradford BD15 7HA
Tel: 0274 547294

Mixed
Age: any age
Bed spaces: 16

Project for drug users who want to explore the
possibilities facing them. Accepts residents on
bail and conditions of bail. Drug-free on
admission. Facilities for pregnant women and
women with babies or children. Access for
less abled people.

Pheonix House
Westoe Drive
South Shields NE33 3EW
Tel: 091 454 5544

Mixed
Age: 18+
Bed spaces: 40 (on 4 sites)

Residential therapeutic community. Drug-and
alcohol-free three days before admission. Will
accept couples.

Phoenix House Sheffield
229 Graham Road
Ranmoor
Sheffield S10 3GS
Tel: 0742 308230/308391

Mixed
Age: 18+
Bed spaces: 47, plus 5 children (on 4 sites)

Residential therapeutic community. Drug-free
24 hours before admission. Trent region and
closely related areas. Operates a small unit for
women and young children or babies.

THE NORTH WEST

Birchwood
Merseyside Drugs Council
23–35 Balls Road
Oxton
Birkenhead
Tel: 051 653 4266

Mixed
Age: 18–30 approx
Bed spaces: 14

Structured self-catering community
particularly aimed at younger people.
Programme length, six months plus. Drug-free
48–72 hours before admission, urine tests
undertaken. Cannot accommodate children or
couples. Will accept people with 'condition of
residence' order.

Chatterton Hey
Edenfield
Ramsbotham
Near Bury
Lancashire

Men only
Age: 18+
Bed spaces: 14

Residential rehabilitation house with Christian philosophy. Drug-free on admission. Referrals through Langley House Trust, 26 Heaton Grove, Bradford. Tel: 0274 496838.

Inward House
89 King Street
Lancaster
(First stage house)

Mixed
Age: 16+
Bed spaces: 22

Highfield View House
Quernmore Road
Lancaster
(Second/third stage house)
Tel: 0524 37519

Residential therapeutic community with structured, hierarchical programme. Drug-free on admission. Self- or other referral.

Phoenix House
The Priory
Bidston
Wirral
Tel: 051 652 2667/3289

Mixed
Age: 16–45
Bed spaces: 32

Residential therapeutic community. Drug-free 24 hours before admission. Preference given to referrals from the North West, but referrals from any area will be considered. Cannot accommodate children but will take couples. People with 'condition of residence' order accepted.

WALES

The Rhoserchan Project
Capel Seion
Aberystwyth
Dyfed SY23 4ED
Tel: 0970 611127

Mixed
Age: 16–65
Bed spaces: 12

Two to six months programme based on the first five of the 12 steps of Alcoholics Anonymous and Narcotics Anonymous. Drug-free on entry: can arrange detoxification. Cannot accommodate children or couples. Do *not* take people with 'condition of residence' order but do take people on a deferred sentence.

Ty Glyn
109 St Mary Street
Cardiff CF1 1DX
Tel: 0222 237947

Mixed
Age: 18+
Bed spaces: 5

Accommodation in a supportive setting for drug users who have been through the first stage of rehabilitation. 12–18 month stay. Three months drug-free before admission. Will accept people 'on condition of residence' order. Cannot accept couples or children.

Ty Palmyra (formerly Emlyn House)
3 Palmyra Place
Newport
Gwent NP9 4EJ
Tel: 0633 263185

Mixed
Age: 18–50
Bed spaces: 19

Seven days drug-free on admission. Cannot accommodate children or couples. People with 'condition of residence' order are *not* accepted although people directed by probation officer *are* accepted.

SCOTLAND

Aberlour Child Care Trust
5 Scarrel Road
Castlemilk
Glasgow G45 0DR
Tel: 041 631 1504

Women and children
Age: Women no limit, children under 12
Bed spaces: 6 women, 12 children

Catchment area: Strathclyde.

Aberlour Child Care Trust
Brenda House
9 Hay Road
Niddrie
Edinburgh
Tel: 031 669 6676

Short stay rehabilitation centres for mothers with their children. Follow up service also available.

The Place
200 Balmore Road
Possil Park
Glasgow
G22 6LJ
Tel: 041 336 8147

Mixed
Age: 16+
Bed spaces: 6

Crisis intervention unit for drug users. Initial stay four to six weeks for detoxification. Additional three weeks may be allowed to arrange community support or referral to longer term residential care.

Roberton House
1 Lancaster Crescent
Glasgow G12 0RR
Tel: 041 334 1118

Mixed
Age: 16+
Bed spaces: 12

Catchment area: Strathclyde. Not necessary to be drug-free on admission but 'functional'. Married couples may be referred. Individual counselling and group therapy.

A-Z
DRUG ABUSERS'
SLANG

A–Z OF DRUG ABUSERS' SLANG

Drug misuse, with the vast number of substances being abused, their varying effects and the different methods of administration, is not an easy subject to grasp. To complicate matters further, users have developed a language all of their own to describe drugs, drug paraphernalia and the progressive stages of administration, effect and withdrawal.

Just like the drugs scene itself, it is a changing language and on occasions peculiar to the drugs sub-culture of one local area.

Parents should realise that young people may use these terms to communicate with fellow users, and at the same time hide their involvement with drugs from others. This is yet another aspect of the drug-taking phenomenon which can seem strange.

The glossary given here is not exhaustive, but it may help in breaking through the language barrier and understanding what is meant when unusual terms are used.

A

A1	Amphetamine
ABBOTS	Barbiturates
ACAPULCO GOLD	Cannabis
ACE	Cannabis cigarette
ACID	LSD
ACID CAP	LSD
ACID HEAD	Regular user of LSD
ADAM	MDMA (ecstasy)
AFGHAN	Cannabis
AFGHAN BLACK	Cannabis
AFRICAN BUSH	Herbal cannabis
ALIAMBA	PCP
AMP	Ampoule
AMPHETS	Amphetamine
ANGEL DRINK	Marijuana alkaloid wine

ANGEL DUST	PCP
ANGELS	Alkyl nitrites
ANGELS	Amytal
ANGELS	Sodium crystals
APPLE	Non-addict
AURORA BOREALIS	PCP

B

BACKTRACK	To withdraw the plunger of needle drawing blood into the syringe
BACKWARDS	A relapse
BAD TRIP	Bad experience from LSD
BAG	Container for drugs
BAGMAN	Drug supplier
BANANAS	Amyl nitrite
BANG	To inject drugs
BANGER	Hypodermic needle
BANGING	Under the influence of drugs
BAR	Cannabis
BARB FREAK	Barbiturate user
BARBS	Barbiturates
BASE	Coca paste
BASE	Cocaine freebase/crack
BASEBALL	Cocaine freebase/crack
BASUCO	Coca paste
BEAM ME UP SCOTTY	PCP/cocaine mix
BEANS	Amphetamine
BEAT	To swindle someone out of drugs or money
BENDER	Drug orgy
BENT	Addicted
BERNICE	Cocaine
BHANG	Cannabis
BIG BROWN ONES	MDMA (ecstasy)
BIG C	Cocaine
BIG HARRY	Heroin
BIG JOHN	The police
BIG MAN	Drug supplier
BILLY	Amphetamine
BILLY WHIZZ	Amphetamine
BINDLE	A number of 'decks' fastened together
BIRDS	Amytal
BIZ	Equipment for injecting
BLACK	Cannabis resin

BLACK MOLLIES	Amphetamine
BLACK ROCK	Cannabis
BLACK ROCK	Crack
BLACK RUSSIAN	Cannabis resin
BLACK STUFF	Opium
BLANKS	Drugs of poor quality
BLAST	Smoke cannabis
BLASTED	Under influence of drugs
BLAW	Cannabis
BLIM	Small pieces of cannabis
BLOCKBUSTERS	Barbiturates
BLOCKED	Under influence of drugs
BLOCKERS	Barbiturates
BLOND HASH	Cannabis
BLOW	Smoke cannabis
BLOW A STICK	Smoke cannabis
BLOW OUT	Spoil an injection
BLUES	Diethylpropion
BLUE ANGEL	Barbiturates
BLUE BANDS	Barbiturates
BLUE BULLETS	Barbiturates
BLUE DEVILS	Barbiturates
BLUE DOLLS	Barbiturates
BLUE HEAVEN	Amytal
BLUE HEAVENS	Alkyl nitrites
BLUE STAR	LSD
BOMBED	High on drugs
BOMBER	Large cannabis cigarette
BOMBIDO	Amphetamine in injectable form
BOMBITA	Amphetamine
BOMBITA	Methylamphetamine
BONGS	Glass smoking pipes
BOO	Cannabis
BOXED	In prison
BRASS	Cannabis
BRICK	A kilogram of cannabis
BRICK	Cannabis
BRIEF	Warrant to arrest or search
BROCCOLI	Cannabis
BUBBLEGUM	Coca paste
BUDDHA GRASS	Cannabis
BUDS	Alkyl nitrites
BUFF	Money
BUGGER	Mexican black tar heroin
BULL	Police officer
BULLET	Capsule

BUMBLE BEES	Amphetamine
BUMMER	Bad experience from LSD
BUN	Quantity of cannabis resin — one kilogram or half a kilogram
BURGERS	MDMA (ecstasy)
BURN	Cheat someone out of drugs or drugs money
BURNED	To receive bad drugs
BUSH	Cannabis
BUSINESS	Injecting equipment
BUSINESSMAN'S TRIP	Methylamphetamine
BUST	Police raid or arrest
BUSY BEE	PCP
BUTTER	Marijuana
(a) BUY	Purchase of drugs by an undercover police officer
BUZY BEE	PCP
BUZZ	Effect induced by taking drugs

C

C	Cocaine
CALIFORNIAN SUNSHINE	LSD
CANADIAN BLACK	Cannabis
CANDY	Barbiturates
CANDY	Cocaine
CANNED	To be arrested
CANNED SATIVA	Cannabis resin
CAP	Capsule
CARAMELLO EGGS	Cannabis resin
CARRIE	Cocaine
CARRIER	Drugs distributor
CARTWHEELS	Amphetamine sulphate
CATCH UP	To withdraw from drugs
CECIL	Cocaine
CHA	Cocaine
CHALK	Methylamphetamine
CHAMP	A drug user who will not reveal his source
CHARAS	Cannabis
CHARGE	Cannabis
CHARGED UP	Under the influence of drugs
CHARLIE	Cocaine
CHARLIE COKE	Cocaine
CHARLIE GIRL	Cocaine

CHASING	Inhaling heroin
CHASING THE DRAGON	Smoking heroin
CHERA	Hashish
CHEWIES	Tuinal
CHI	Heroin
CHICKEN POWDER	Amphetamine
CHINA WHITE	Fentanyl
CHINA WHITE	Heroin
CHINESE H	Heroin
CHIPPERS	Occasional heroin user
CHITARI	Cannabis
CHOLLY	Cocaine
CHRIS	Methylamphetamine
CHRISTMAS TREES	Amphetamine
CHRISTMAS TREES	Barbiturates
CHRISTY	Methylamphetamine
CLEAR UP	To withdraw from drugs
CLOUD 9	Crack
COASTING	Under the influence of drugs
COCA PASTE	An intermediate product in the processing of the coca leaf into cocaine
COKE	Cocaine
COKED UP	Under the influence of cocaine
COKIE	Cocaine addict
COLD TURKEY	Withdraw from drugs
COME DOWN	Withdrawal effects
(to) CONNECT	To buy drugs
CONNECTION	Drug supplier
COOK UP	Making crack from cocaine hydrochloride
COOK UP	Prepare for an injection
COOK UP A PILL	Prepare opium for smoking
COOL SMOKE	Refers to smoking 'ice'
CO-PILOTS	Amphetamine
CO-PILOTS	Take LSD with another
CORINE	Cocaine
COTICS	Narcotics
CRACK	A form of cocaine that can be smoked
CRANK	Amphetamine
CRANK	Crack
CRANK	Methylamphetamine
CRANKING UP	Injecting drugs
CROKER	Doctor
CROKER JOINT	Hospital

CROSSROADS	Amphetamine
CRYSTAL	Methylamphetamine
CRYSTAL METH	Methylamphetamine
CRYSTALS	Amphetamine
CUBE	Cube of morphine
CUNG	Cannabis
CUT/CUTTING	Mixing drug with other substances (usually non-drug) to increase quantity

D

DAGGA	Cannabis
DDU	Drug Dependency Unit
DEALER	Supplier of drugs
DECK	A small packet of drugs
DETOX	Withdrawing of drugs under medical supervision
DEX	Dexedrine
DEXIES	Dexedrine
DEXY	Dexedrine
DFs	DF 118s
DIBBLE	Police
DIET PILLS	Amphetamine
DIKE	Diconal
DIRTY	Cannabis
DIRTY MONEY	Money from drugs/crime
DISCO BISCUITS	MDMA (ecstasy)
DOLLIES	Methadone
DOLLS	Methadone
DOPE	Cannabis
DOUBLE DREADS	Amphetamine and LSD mixture
DOUBLE TROUBLE	Tuinal
DOUBLE ZERO	Hashish
DOUBLECROSS	Amphetamine
DOVES	MDMA tablets (ecstasy)
DOWNERS	Barbiturates
DRAGON	Heroin
DRAW	Cannabis
DREAMER	Morphine
DRIPPER	Eye-dropper
DROP	Take LSD
DROPPED	Arrested
DRY HIGH	Cannabis
DS	Drug squad

DUBBE	Cannabis
DUBY	Cannabis
DUMMY	Poor quality drugs
DUST	Cocaine
DUST	PCP
DYNAMITE	Mixture of cocaine and morphine

E

E	MDMA (ecstasy)
EGGS	Temazepam capsules
EIGHT BALLS	Crack
EIGHTH	Eighth of an ounce
ECSTASY	Amphetamine-type drug with hallucinogenic effects — MDMA
EKIES	MDMA (ecstasy)
ELEPHANT	Heroin
ELEPHANT TRANQUILLISER	PCP
EMBALMING FLUID	PCP
EYE OPENERS	Amphetamines

F

F-40s	Barbiturates
FALL	To be arrested
FANTASIA	MDMA (ecstasy)/mescaline
FAST	Amphetamine sulphate
FINGERS	Cannabis resin
FINK	Informant
FIX	Injecting drugs
FIXED	Under influence of drugs
FIXING	Injecting drugs
FLAKE	Crack
FLASHBACKS	Hallucinations which occur sometime later after regular use of hallucinogens
FLEA POWDER	Poor quality drugs
FLOATING	Under the influence of drugs
FLYING	Under the influence of drugs
FLYING SAUCERS	Morning Glory seeds
(to) FOLD UP	To withdraw from drugs
FOOTBALLS	Amphetamine
FREAKING OUT	Bad experience from LSD
FREEBASE	Crack
FREEBASING	Smoking cocaine
FREEZE	Cocaine

FRENCH BLUES	Amphetamines
FRONT/FRONT MONEY	Money in advance to pay for drugs

G

GAGE	Cannabis
GANGA	Cannabis
GANGSTER	Cannabis
GEAR	Drugs — refers particularly to heroin
GEEZE	Injection of narcotics
GERONIMO	Alcohol/barbiturate mix
GHANJA	Cannabis
GIGGLEWEED	Cannabis
GIMMICKS	Equipment for injecting
GIRL	Cocaine
GLASS	Methylamphetamine (ice)
GLASS BROWNIES	Cannabis
GO	Methylamphetamine
GOLD DUST	Cocaine
GOLD STAR	Cocaine
GOOFBALLS	Barbiturates
GOON CRYSTAL	PCP
GORILLA PILLS	Barbiturates
GRASS	Herbal cannabis
GRAVEL	Crack
GREEN DRAGONS	Barbiturates
GREENIES	Amphetamine
GREY BISCUITS	MDMA (ecstasy)
GRIFFO	Cannabis
GROOVE	Having a good time on drugs
GROOVING	Having a good time on drugs
GUM	Opium
GUN	Equipment for injecting

H

H	Heroin
HABIT	User's drug need — usually referring to those who have become addicted
HALF	Half an ounce
HALF LOAD	15 decks of heroin
HALLOO-WACH	Amphetamine
HAMBURGERS	MDMA (ecstasy)
HANDBALL	Crack

(to) HANG UP	To withdraw from drugs
HAPPY DUST	Cocaine
HARD STUFF	Morphine
HARRY	Heroin
HASH	Cannabis resin
HASH OIL	Cannabis
HASHISH	Cannabis resin
HAY	Cannabis
HEAD	Person addicted to drugs
HEARTS	Amphetamine
HEELED	Possession of drugs or a weapon
HEMP	Cannabis
HERB J	Cannabis
HIGH	Under the influence of drugs
HIGH TEC	Alkyl nitrites
HIT	Injection
(to) HIT	To buy drugs
HO	Cannabis
HOG	PCP
HOMEBAKE	Heroin
HOOKED	To be addicted
HOP	Opium
HOPHEAD	A narcotic addict
HORSE	Heroin
HOTLOAD	Overdose, which may be fatal
HOTSMOKE	Refers to smoking crack
HUFFING	Misusing solvents/volatile substances
HUG DRUG	MDMA (ecstasy)
HYPERJACKS	Ampoules

I

ICE	Cocaine
ICE	Crystal methylamphetamine
ICECREAM HABIT	Irregular drug habit
IDIOT PILLS	Barbiturates
INDIAN CANNABIS	Cannabis
INDIAN HEMP	Cannabis

J

JAB	Inject drugs
JACK	Heroin tablet
JACK UP	Injecting drugs
JACKING UP	Injecting drugs

JANE	Cannabis
JIVE	Cannabis
JOINT	Cannabis cigarette
JOLT	Inject drugs into vein
JOY	Heroin
JOY POWDER	Heroin or cocaine
JUGGED	To be arrested
JUGGLE	An addict selling drugs to finance his own habit
JUNK	Heroin
JUNKER	Heroin addict
JUNKIE	Drug addict

K

K	Ketamine hydrochloride
KAJEES	Cannabis
KEE	One kilogram of drugs
KICK	Effect of drug, particularly a stimulant
(to) KICK	To abandon drug habit
KIEF	Cannabis
KIF	Cannabis
KING KONG PILLS	Barbiturates
KIT	Drug addict's equipment or paraphernalia
KITT	Cannabis
KJ	PCP

L

LADY	Cocaine
LADY	Glassware for smoking cocaine
LAUNDERING MONEY	A process to hide the criminal source of money and to make it appear legitimate
LAY ON/LAID ON	Supply drugs on deferred payment
LEAF	Cocaine
LEBANESE	Cannabis resin
LEBANESE GOLD	Cannabis
LEMON	Poor quality drugs
LEMONADE	Poor quality drugs
LIDO	Crack
LIGHTNING	Amphetamine
LINE	Quantity of amphetamine or cocaine

LIQUID GOLD	Alkyl nitrites
LIT UP	Under the influence of drugs
LOCO WEED	Cannabis
LOPPY DUST	Cocaine
LOVE DOVES	MDMA (ecstasy)
LOVE WEED	Cannabis
LOZ	One ounce of cannabis

M

M	Morphine
M25	MDMA (ecstasy)
MACHINERY	Equipment for injecting
MACKA	Amphetamine
MAGIC MUSHROOMS	Mushrooms that cause hallucinations
MAINLINE	Injecting drugs intravenously
MAKE THE TURN	To withdraw from drugs
MALAWI COB	Cannabis in the shape of a cigar
MALAWI GRASS	Cannabis
MAN	Source of supply — dealer
MARSHMALLOW	Barbiturates
MARSHMALLOW REDS	Barbiturates
MARY	Cannabis
MEET	A meeting between drug users and suppliers
METH	Methylamphetamine
METH AMPS	MDMA (ecstasy)
MEXICAN BROWN	Heroin
MEXICAN GREEN	Cannabis
MEXICAN REDS	Barbiturates
MEZZ	Cannabis
MINIBERRIES	Amphetamine
MISS EMMA	Morphine
MISSILE	PCP
MOGGIES	Mogadon
MOHASKY	Cannabis
MOJO	Narcotics
MONF	Morphine
MONKEY	Morphine
(to have) MONKEY ON THE BACK	To be addicted
MORAGRIFA	Cannabis
MORF	Morphine
MOROCCAN (GOLD)	Cannabis resin
MOTHER'S LITTLE HELPER	Barbiturates
(playing the) MOUTH-ORGAN	Using a matchbox cover to 'chase the dragon'

MOW THE GRASS	Smoke cannabis
MUD	Methadone
MULE	Carrier of drugs for another — usually over international borders
MUTAH	Cannabis

N

NAIL	Needle
NAILED	To be arrested
NEB	Barbiturates
NECKING	Swallowing drugs to avoid detection
NEPALESE (BLACK)	Cannabis resin
NEW YORKERS	MDMA (ecstasy) — large white tablets
NIMBY	Barbiturates
NOSE CANDY	Cocaine
NUGGETS	Crystals of cocaine

O

O	Opium
OD	Overdose
OFF YOUR FACE	High on drugs
OLJA	Cannabis
ON A TRIP	Under the influence of a hallucinogenic drug
ON ICE	In prison
ON THE BRICKS	Released from prison
ON THE NOD	Under the influence of drugs
ONE	Cannabis oil
ORANGES	Dexedrine tablets
ORBIT	MDMA (ecstasy)
OUTFIT	Drug addict's equipment or paraphernalia
OVER AND UNDER	A combination of a stimulant and depressant drug
OZONE	PCP

P

PAKI (BLACK)	Cannabis resin
PANAMA RED	Cannabis
PANIC	Shortage of drugs
PAPER	Prescription
PAPER MUSHROOMS	LSD

PARACHUTE	Crack mixed with heroin
PARADISE	Cocaine
PASS	A transfer of drugs or money
PASTA	Coca paste
PEACE PILL	PCP
PEACHES	Amphetamine
PEANUTS	Barbiturates
PEARLY GATES	Morning Glory seeds
PEDDLER	Seller of drugs
PEEP	PCP
PEP PILLS	Amphetamine
PERCY	Small amount of drugs for personal use
PETH	Pethidine
PHYAMPS	Methadone
PIECE	Container for drugs
PILLHEAD	Amphetamine user
PINK LADIES	Barbiturates
PINK STUDS	MDMA (ecstasy)
PINKS	Seconal
PINNED	Description of constricted pupils after consuming heroin
PITZU	Impure morphine base
PLANT	Hiding place or cache of drugs
POD	Cannabis
POISON	Heroin
POOR MAN'S COCAINE	Methylamphetamine
POP	To inject drugs
POPPERS	Alkyl nitrites
POPPING (PILLS)	Swallowing drugs in pill form
POT	Cannabis
POWDER	Heroin
PUFF	Smoke cannabis
PULVER	Amphetamine
PURE	Good quality, high purity drugs
PUSH	To sell drugs
PUSHER	Seller of drugs

Q

QUARTER	Quarter of an ounce
QUARTER MOON	Cannabis resin
QUICK SILVER	Alkyl nitrites
QUILL	A matchbox cover, may be folded, used for sniffing (snorting) narcotics

R

RAINBOWS	Tuinal
RAM	Alkyl nitrites
RAVE	Acid house party or pay party
READER	Prescription
RED AND BLUES	Tuinal
RED BIRDS	Seconal
RED DEVILS	Barbiturates
RED DEVILS	Methylamphetamine
RED ROCK	Methadone
RED SEAL	Cannabis resin
REDS	Seconal
REDS AND BLUES	Barbiturates
REEFER	Cannabis cigarette
RESIN	Cannabis
RITIES	Ritalin
ROACH	Butt of cannabis cigarette
ROCK CRANK	Methylamphetamine
ROCKS	Heroin or crack
ROCKY	Cannabis resin
ROPE	Marijuana
ROSES	Amphetamine
ROXANNE	Crack
ROYALTY	Cocaine
RUMBLE	Police search or inquiry
RUSH	Alkyl nitrites
RUSH	The euphoric effect of a drug on the user

S

SATIVA	Cannabis
SCAG	Heroin
SCAT	Heroin
SCENE	The drugs environment
SCHOOL BOY	Codeine
SCORE	To buy drugs
SCRATCH	Money
SCRIPT	Prescription
SECIES	Seconal
SEGGY	Seconal
SENSE	Cannabis Sinsemilla
SERPICO	Crack
SHERMANS	PCP
SHIT	Cannabis

SHOOTING GALLERY	A meeting place for addicts where they inject drugs
SHOOTING UP	Injecting drugs
SHOT DOWN	Under the influence of drugs
SKAG	Heroin
SKIN	Cigarette papers
SKIN POPPING	Injecting just under the skin
SLEEPERS	Barbiturates
SLEEPING PILLS	Barbiturates
SLEIGH-RIDE	Cocaine
SMACK	Cocaine
SMACK	Heroin
SMILEY	LSD capsules/tablets
SMOKE	Cannabis
SNAPPERS	Alkyl nitrites
SNIFFING	Inhaling amphetamines or cocaine
SNORTING	Consuming cocaine by sniffing through the nose
SNOW	Cocaine
SNOWBALLING	Injecting or sniffing a mixture of heroin and cocaine
SNOWTOKE	Crack
SOAP	Block of cannabis shaped like a tablet of soap
SOFTBALLS	Barbiturates
SOLES	Cannabis resin
SPACE BASE	PCP with cocaine
SPEED	Amphetamine
SPEEDBALLING	Injecting or sniffing a mixture of heroin and cocaine
SPEEDBALLS	Heroin mixed with cocaine
SPECIAL K	Ketamine hydrochloride
SPIKE	Hypodermic needle
SPLASH	Amphetamine
SPLIFF	Cannabis cigarette
SPOON	Sixteenth of an ounce
SPUTNIK	Opium mixed with Pakistani cannabis
SQUARE	Non-addict
STARDUST	Cocaine
STASH	Drug dealer's hiding place
STICKS	Cannabis
STONED	Under the influence of drugs
(to be) STRUNG OUT	Addicted
STUFF	Cannabis and heroin

STUFFER	A smuggler who conceals drugs in the vagina or anus to avoid detection
STUMBLERS	Barbiturates
SUGAR	LSD
SULPH	Amphetamine sulphate
SULPHATES	Amphetamine in powder form
SUPERCLOUD	Crack
SUPERWHITE	Crack
SWALLOWER	A person who swallows drugs (e.g. in a condom) to avoid detection
SWEETS	Amphetamine

T

T	Cannabis
TAB	Tablet or quantity of drug (usually LSD)
TAKE A TRIP	Take LSD
TAKROURI	Cannabis
TANGO AND CASH	Heroin
TAR	Opium or morphine
TASTE	A sample of drugs
TEA	Cannabis
TEMAZIES	Temazepam capsules
TEMMIES	Temazepam tablets
TEMPLE BALLS	Cannabis
TEXAS TEA	Cannabis
THAI STICKS	Cannabis
THING	Heroin
THRUSTERS	Amphetamine
TIC AND TAC	PCP
TIGER	Heroin
TOFFEE WHIZZ	Amphetamine
TOOLS	Equipment for injecting
TOOT	Cocaine
TOOTING	Smoking heroin or other drugs through a tube
TOOTSIE ROLL	Methadone
TORCH UP	Light up cannabis cigarette
TORNADO	Crack
TOSS	Search a person or premises
TOTE	A smoke of heroin
TRACKING	Injecting intravenously along a vein
TRANX	Tranquillisers

TRAVEL AGENT	Street drug dealer
TRIP	Effect induced by taking hallucinogens
TRIPS	LSD
TRUCK DRIVERS	Amphetamine
TURKEY	Poor quality drugs or non-drug substance used to deceive
TURN A DRUM OVER	Police search of a house
TURNABOUTS	Amphetamine
TURNED OFF	Withdrawn from drugs
TURNED ON	Under the influence of drugs

U

UPPERS	Amphetamine and stimulants generally
UPS	Amphetamine

W

WACKY-BACKY	Cannabis resin
WAKE-AMINE	Amphetamine
WAKE UPS	Amphetamine
WALLPAPER	Money
WASCH	Cannabis resin
WASH	Crack
WASHED ROCK	Freebase cocaine
WASHED UP	Withdrawn from drugs
WASHING	Preparing crack
WASTED	Under the influence of drugs
WEED	Cannabis
WEEDHEAD	Marijuana abuser
WEEKEND HABIT	Irregular habit
WEST COAST TURN AROUNDS	Amphetamine
WHITE CLOUD	Crack
WHITE DOVES	MDMA (ecstasy) tablets
WHITE DYNAMITE	Heroin
WHITE GIRL	Cocaine
WHITE STUFF	Cocaine
WHITES	Amphetamine sulphate tablets
WHIZZ	Amphetamine sulphate
WHIZZ	Tablets impregnated with LSD
WHIZZ BOMBS	MDMA (ecstasy)
WIRED TO THE MOON	High on drugs

WORKS	Apparatus for injecting
WRAP	Street quantity of drugs (heroin, amphetamine, cocaine) sold in small folded paper bags or foil packets
WRECKED	High on drugs

X

XTC	MDMA (ecstasy)

Y

YELLOW CALLIES	MDMA (ecstasy)
YELLOW SUBMARINES	Temazepam
YELLOWS	Barbiturates
YESCA	Cannabis

Z

ZANI	Cannabis
ZIP	Methylamphetamine
ZOOM	A mixture of cocaine, heroin and amphetamine which is either sniffed or injected